PAUL J. BATURA

Tyndale House Publishers, Inc., Wheaton, Illinois

Visit Tyndale's exciting Web site at www.tyndale.com

Designed by Jessie McGrath

Library of Congress Cataloging-in-Publication Data

Batura, Paul J.
    p. cm.
    Includes bibliographical references.
    ISBN 1-4143-0134-0 (hc)
    1. Dobson, James C., date. 2. Child psychologists—United States—Biography. 3. Focus on the Family (Organization)—Biography. 4. Conservatism—Religious aspects—Christianity. 5. Christianity and politics—United States. I. Title.
    BR1725.D62B38 2004
    269'.2'092—dc22   2004015273

Printed in the United States of America.

10 09 08 07 06 05 04
9   8   7   6   5   4   3   2   1

*To my mom and dad, Joan and Jim Batura,
whose gentle and loving hands of influence remain on
my life no matter how far from childhood I travel.
Because of the Christian principles first exemplified
for me in our home, I am able to recognize and
appreciate godly leadership in others.*

TABLE OF CONTENTS

OVER THE COURSE OF THIS WRITING, I was reminded that the success of a single project rests on the shoulders of many. To quote the lovable and laudable angel Clarence in *It's a Wonderful Life,* "One man's life touches so many others—when he's not there it leaves an awfully big hole." Indeed, *Gadzooks!* rests in your hands today because of the collective effort of the many kindhearted people who took the time to invest in this unique study of Dr. James C. Dobson.

Foremost is my favorite person in all the world—my beautiful wife, Julie. She read every word of the manuscript, constructively editing, suggesting—and, most of all, encouraging—from beginning to end. As I retreated to our home office to write, she would often settle into her music room, unknowingly serenading me with such absolute magnificence that, as a result, I often felt that my prose would "sing" when it might otherwise have sunk!

When I first approached my boss about this project, Dr. Dobson graciously gave me what every young and aspiring writer needs most: a chance to see if he has what it takes to get published. Thank you, Doctor, for believing and trusting in me; by far, you are the best teacher I never had in the classroom, exhibiting by simple example the deep and eternal lessons found in a life well lived.

My friends at Tyndale House have personified professionalism. Many have touched this endeavor under my radar, but I welcome the opportunity to thank those I know personally. To Doug Knox, for exhibiting confidence in my abilities; to Janis Long Harris, for tolerating—and answering—my endless series of questions; to Sharon Leavitt, for offering a hand of friendship; to Gail Castle, for being so pleasant to talk with regardless of how stressful the day might have been; to Caleb Sjogren, for so kindly facilitating the final yet crucial details of the project; and to Stephanie Voiland, for her eagle eye—in the words of Sheriff Andy Taylor: "Much obliged!"

In school, one always hears that a writer is only as good as is his editor. Lisa Jackson's genius and talents attest that adage is true! From one marathoner to another—your willingness to put in the miles helps make this finish sweeter still.

Diana Vanse and Alice Crider sat with Julie and me for several hours one Sunday afternoon—all for the cost of a cup of coffee—explaining the terms of my publishing contract. How I appreciate their willingness to help me as I got my feet wet in this new and exciting world.

To my cohorts of the "Wing" at Focus on the Family—Sherry Hoover, Diana Ginn, Terri Lempuhl, Corinne Sayler, Gail Hinson, and Claide Marauri—what a perspective you give through your selfless service and wonderful attitude. Though we may not party as often as the boss seems to think we do, your presence and partnership throughout the day are gifts for which I am most grateful. To Ron Reno—I count your steady hand of leadership and discernment to be tops and worthy of note. Thank you for allowing me to bounce so many ideas off of you and for taking the time to so carefully review the material.

To my running buddies—David "the Berv" Bervig, Al "Two-Runs-a-Day" DeLaRoche, and Marlen "the Chief" Wells—it is difficult to quantify how helpful you have been to me. First, to the Berv—your trust set in motion not only my career, but my personal life as well! You've heard the contents of this book every which way from Sunday during our lunchtime runs, yet you still promised to read it. To Al, a man of great wisdom who has a penchant for knowing when to talk and when to remain silent—your familiarity with Dr. Dobson has been of immeasurable wealth to me. Finally, to Marlen, whose friendship came amidst the fire of a time of great testing—your wonderful wit, combined with our mutual love and respect for our founder and chairman, inspired me to see many of the profound and poignant lessons found within the simple stories of Dr. Dobson's life.

Many men and women took the time to offer their perspectives, memories, and thoughts surrounding life within the walls of Focus on the Family. I especially appreciate Don and Barbara Hodel's insight, Dr. H. B. London's kindness and levity, Gary Lydic's enthusiasm and wisdom, Ron Wilson's passion, Diane Passno's ability to articulate the essence of who Dr. Dobson is, Paul Hetrick's discerning wit and ability to weave a story without missing a detail, and Patty Watkins's knack for finding humor in the stressful. Dr. Dobson's security detail—Bruce Hoover, Mike Benzie, Den Patterson, Sam Moore, and Brian Roland—offered a tremendous perspective otherwise hidden from public view. Del Tackett's reflections, Karen Bethany's reminisces, Robert Wolgemuth's viewpoint, and Jim Davis's yarns and jocularity—these are but a fraction of the contributions that enabled me to show rather than tell about Dr. Dobson's unique principles of leadership and life.

May God bless these wonderful colleagues and friends.

"Not by might nor by power, but by my Spirit,"
says the Lord Almighty.
ZECHARIAH 4:6

GADZOOKS?

{gad-'züks\ interjection\ archaic: an expression of surprise; a mild oath}

At times, fact finds its way into both lore and legend. The story behind my first exposure to *Gadzooks!* happens to be one of those times. Since my first position at Focus on the Family was in the marketing division, my contact with Dr. James Dobson, Focus on the Family's chairman and founder, was infrequent. The old-timers peppered me with stories of how wonderfully tough he was to work with, expending the energy of a man half his age. One long-time employee told me that Dr. Dobson burned the bulbs out in his office twice as fast as everyone else because of the hours he kept. Another told me he was so concerned with answering every piece of mail that he even required the correspondence department to acknowledge "Dear Occupant" letters. They would tell me how he paid attention to the slightest detail—from the length of the grass on campus to the length of time it took for a team member to answer the phone (a three-ring maximum!). Conceptually, I could believe it, but practically, I just didn't see it because I didn't see much of him—at first.

I would occasionally see him passing in the hall, sitting in the broadcast studio, or speaking at our monthly chapel service. Always the gracious gentleman, he seemed to glide from place to place with an elegant ease. To me, he appeared like a patriarchal grandfather with a warm smile that could melt even the coldest glare. And although he had a reputation for never backing away from an ideological battle, he struck me as a man immune to irritation. It seemed to be beneath him. He gave the impression that he was less interested in the detail than he was in the final score of the game. But I would quickly learn that to Dr. James Dobson, the quality of the playbook is often the best predictor of victory.

THE MEMO

It arrived innocently enough in a tattered, well-used, interoffice envelope. Taking it from my department mailbox, I casually walked back to my cubicle as my fingers unwound the string that sealed the package. Sliding the single sheet of paper out, I could see that it was a copy of a memo I had written just one day earlier.

Only a few months on the job, I had made a mistake and sent five hundred people two copies of the same letter. It was a careless error. Asked by my supervisor how this had happened, I penned a rather pathetic explanation. Rife with speculative commentary, the memorandum offered an exhaustive list of possible scenarios involving various people and departments outside of my purview that could have possibly, though unlikely, led to the blunder in question. Only in the concluding paragraph did I finally offer an admission of guilt—and it came grudgingly at that! Filled with dry, corporate lingo, my memo could have come directly from a Dilbert comic strip. Somehow this backhanded mea culpa had found its way to James Dobson's office—and back again to me.

With a fine felt-tip pen, Dr. Dobson had scrawled diagonally across the memo the following message:

GADZOOKS! Institutional stench!
Please be more careful! JCD

My first correspondence with the founder of the organization—and he had referenced my writing as "institutional stench." Perfect. What a way to launch a career in ministry!

ORIGIN

According to linguists, the term *gadzooks* originated from a mispronunciation of "God's hooks." What once referenced the nails used in the Crucifixion is now considered a benign, colorful exclamation, a reference to large quantities of homegrown zucchini, or a Dallas-based clothing store for teenagers. Strange, but true.

Within the ranks of Focus on the Family, it's a word you hope not to see on a memo or report.

That's because within the word *gadzooks* hangs a heavy and emotional message from Dr. James Dobson. In short, it means this: You blew it; you made a mistake; you let someone down; you weren't thinking a step ahead—*if* you were thinking at all. In deeper terms, it means this: Jesus Christ was not glorified as a result of this action; the gospel was hindered; sacrificial giving was not honored; the integrity and character of Focus on the Family were compromised.

With a Ph.D. in child development and over forty years of counseling experience, Dr. Dobson is no stranger to what motivates people and how to bring out the best in each person. He knows that a person who can motivate others will likely be more successful in managing the people he leads and the life he lives.

Dr. Dobson has devoted his life to the service of others in the name of Jesus Christ. An author of over twenty best-selling books, his radio program is heard by as many as 200 million people each week from one side of the world to the other. For over thirty years, he has offered biblically based counsel on topics ranging from marriage to parenting to hundreds of other family-related issues. He has served four of the last five presidential administrations.

Despite an ever-changing culture, much of the advice he offers has been as timeless as the tides. Rooted in both solid science and the divinely inspired Word of God, Dr. Dobson's methods have proven effective. His words have aided parents, comforted couples, and even frustrated some kids, as this recent letter to our office can attest. Scrawled in crayon, this disgruntled six-year-old wrote:

> DEAR DOBONSON,
> You are a mean and curle thing. You and your dumb sayings won't take you to Heaven.
>
> SINCERELY,
> *Kristy P.*
>
> P.S. Kids don't like wippens.

James Dobson will tell you that raising the ire of a young child today is a small price to pay if the corrective discipline leads to a more responsible and grounded adult of tomorrow. From his early days of counseling, Dr. Dobson has advocated gentle yet firm remedial measures, like a swat or a spank for children who just won't respond to verbal persuasion. Research has confirmed the effectiveness of this approach, though critics continue to unfairly portray spanking as a mere extension of abuse.

Nonetheless, enough time has passed for Dr. Dobson to see the fruits of this "controversial" viewpoint, and despite the seriousness associated with the topic, he has enjoyed letters like the one below. A few years ago, a college student who was attending Focus on the Family Institute sent a note to our office:

> *Roses are red,*
> *Violets are blue—*
> *I got spanked as a kid—*
> *All because of you!*

Comic relief not withstanding, James Dobson's touch can be felt from one side of the globe to the other and is now influencing a second generation of families. In the beginning, though, nobody could have predicted what has since come to pass.

In almost twenty-seven years, Dr. Dobson's inspiration has grown from a one-room, two-person endeavor into a global ministry with an American team of almost 1,300 staff members. Nearly five thousand people have worked at Focus on the Family since its doors first opened in 1977. Their duties have been numerous and varied. They have answered the phones, opened the mail, prayed for and with the grieving, and rejoiced with those whose prayers have been answered. They have swept the floors, cut the grass, shoveled snow, and cooked meals. They have helped create and produce radio and television programming that's heard and seen in 162 different countries.

Dr. Dobson's vision does not spring from a motivation for money or for the glorification and nourishment of an insatiable ego. Simply put, Focus on the Family exists because he believes that the preservation of the family is critical to the survival of the nation and, ultimately, the propagation of the gospel of Jesus Christ.

This is why Dr. Dobson walked away from a successful career at Childrens Hospital in southern California. This is why he put everything on the line and allowed his feet to follow his faith. And this is why so many people have followed in his footsteps and come to work at Focus on the Family.

I am incredibly blessed to be one of those people.

My current position as Dr. Dobson's personal assistant for research has permitted me to see him up close, day in and day out. With a desk only a few paces from his office, I've watched, heard, and even played a small part in events that have left a mark on history. I've heard phone calls in which he persuaded senators to vote for pro-family legislation; I've seen how radio and television appearances have helped turn enemies and detractors into friends and supporters. I've met giants of the faith, heroes of the country, and great leaders.

In a country where more than half of the workers are dissatisfied at work, I am a very fortunate man. Do I love my job? No. I *like* my job.

I *love* my boss.

I love what he does and does not stand for. I love how he treats friend and foe alike with dignity and respect. I love how he treats a stranger like a friend he's never met. I love that if you know what he cares about, you know how he will react to any situation, at any time, in any place. I love that he is the same man in person as he is on the radio or on television.

However sappy and insincere that may seem at first glance, I assure you, it is the truth. Is Dr. James Dobson perfect? Of course not. Is our office a one-stop fun shop? No. But it is a great place to work and Dr. James Dobson is a great man to work for.

He is a man who leads and lives in paradoxical fashion.

He is very traditional in his beliefs, yet unique in his habits. He is a man of many passions, but at the same time, he's a long-time disciple of self-discipline. What he receives, he is more likely to give away. What he gives away, he often gets back. He is a detailed thinker, yet his actions are visionary in nature. He rarely has a minute to spare in the course of a day but will take an hour to talk with a hurting, single mom or a lonely, elderly man. He is persistent when trying to find a fact but patient with his family and the foibles of his staff. He's a friend of the powerful but a defender of the weak.

This is Dr. James Dobson. This is my boss.

Gadzooks! is a firsthand account of what I've learned working for America's foremost family counselor. It's the story of what I've seen and heard within the walls of his office.

It's the story of how he motivates and inspires those in the mailroom, the boardroom, and every place in between.

While the principles laid out on the following pages may highlight the personal habits of Dr. James Dobson, their source is rooted in the life of Jesus Christ. From the work front to the home front, Dr. Dobson's principles of life and leadership are applicable to anybody, anywhere. May you find them as helpful in your pursuit of personal and professional success as I have.

PRACTICAL PRINCIPLE #1

STOP, DROP, AND ROLL WITH IT

Now here at the Rock we have two rules.
Memorize them until you can say them in
your sleep. Rule number one: Obey all rules.
Rule number two: No writing on the walls.
BARNEY FIFE

By my third and final meeting, I wasn't sure if I'd been inter-viewing for a job as Dr. James Dobson's research assistant or a spot on the U.S. Olympic gymnastics team. On three separate occasions, three different people had asked me three variations of the same question:

"Are you a flexible person?" asked Jackie Kintz of human resources.

"How do you feel about a day that starts in one direction," pressed Ron Reno, the director of the president's office, "yet winds up ending in another?"

And finally, from Dr. Dobson himself: "Paul," he cau-tioned, "the pace in this office can be breathtaking—and there's no question about it, this job will stretch you. Do you think you're up to the challenge?"

In a cautious yet confident tone, I answered affirmatively each time. I quickly learned, however, that within each ques-tion there was a prescient warning of great worth: You'd better

1

be ready to go with the flow or you'll soon discover that the flow will go without you!

In many ways, working in James Dobson's office is very much like living in the average American household. The pace is fast, plans change on a moment's notice, and priorities are often shuffled faster than a deck of cards in Las Vegas! Indeed, in the years since my initial interview, time has taught me that flexibility and adaptability in the workplace may very well be the two main keys to professional success. While the remaining eighteen principles contained within this book are vital and important, they mean very little if your spirit is stubborn or you're unwilling to make adjustments that are in the best interest of your organization.

What I'm saying is this: Flexibility is the hinge on which all the rest of these rules swing. In simpler terms, sometimes you have to stop, drop what you're doing, and roll with what may come.

Consider the circumstances in which the apostles chose to follow Jesus. The Scriptures don't suggest that there was an elaborate application process, or that the twelve were given a written offer and a window of time to weigh the wisdom of the opportunity at hand. Hardly. In the midst of a fishing expedition along the shores of Galilee, four men—Simon, Andrew, James, and John—encountered a Jesus who was in need of a quick answer. "Come, follow me," Jesus said, "and I will make you fishers of men" (Mark 1:17). Did they ask for some time to think about it? No! "At once they left their nets," records Mark, "and followed him" (v. 18). They changed their plans, Jesus changed them, and as a result, they set out to change the world by sharing the teachings of their Master.

God's Word is full of examples where the plans of the Lord necessitate human flexibility. You might recall how the Magi, warned in a dream about Herod's intention to slay the infant Jesus, chose to circumvent the king and travel home by a different route after the birth of Christ (Matthew 2:12).

In Luke, we read that Jesus chastised a woman named Martha who was critical of her sister, Mary, for dropping everything when Christ came to visit. Martha wanted to stay on task—and saw only the unfinished chores of the household. "You are worried and upset about many things, but only one thing is needed. Mary has chosen what is better, and it will not be taken away from her," Jesus said to Martha (Luke 10:41-42). Mary made adjustments—Martha did not. Of course, this isn't all that surprising because as humans we're often resistant to change. In his first letter to the Philippians, the apostle Paul revealed just such a personal struggle. "I am torn between the two," he wrote. "I desire to depart and be with Christ, which is better by far; but it is more necessary for you that I remain in the body" (Philippians 1:23-24). Paul made adjustments, resisted the urge to throw in the towel and, as a result, set in motion a movement unlike any the world had ever seen. Paul understood what many of us quickly forget: God's plans don't change, but ours often need to if we're to live in accordance with Him.

CHANGING ON THE FLY

Have you ever watched a game of hockey? Unlike baseball, basketball, and football, play doesn't halt to accommodate a substitution. At a predetermined time, known only to the respective squad, a "line" of players will skate off the ice and be replaced by a fresh group of teammates. This line shift, however well practiced, often appears chaotic, with inadvertent collisions and mishaps that result in too many or too few players remaining on the ice, or maybe even an opponent being left unguarded. In short, it's the efficiency of the transition—and the capitalization of opportunity when presented—that often determines the success or failure of the team.

Isn't that very much like life itself? Neither opportunity nor adversity can be counted on to give adequate notice. It's our reaction to varying situations, not always the predicament itself, that makes or breaks the circumstance. It's all about adjustment and transition.

In many ways, I liken our office here at Focus on the Family to an NHL ice rink. The clock runs continuously, the opponent moves quickly and unpredictably, the surface is slick, and the barbs from the sidelines can sometimes be brutal. Yet in response, Dr. Dobson is not afraid to pull the goalie in return for an extra skater if we're late in the game and looking to score.

In the summer of 2003, Judge Roy Moore, at the time the chief justice of the Alabama Supreme Court, was ordered by a federal judge to remove a stone display of the Ten Commandments from the rotunda of the Alabama Judicial Building. The judge refused, citing the oath he took upon entering office that invokes God's name, and thus, God's law. Government officials disagreed and stated emphatically that the monument violated the "separation of church and state" tradition. To protest the court order, thousands of citizens began to gather daily on the steps of the Montgomery courthouse to pray and petition the state to leave the two-and-a-half ton granite marker in place. With each passing day, the rallies grew in size.

At the time of the ruling, Dr. Dobson was in Washington, D.C., attending a weeklong series of meetings on the Federal Marriage Amendment. With the removal of the monument imminent, a coalition from Alabama phoned Focus on the Family president Don Hodel, wondering if the ministry, and in particular, James Dobson, would be available to host a rally the next day in Montgomery. Less than twenty-four hours before the rally, Don called Dr. Dobson in Washington. Would he consider attending?

"Let's do it!" said Dr. Dobson. "If not now, then when?" Transportation was quickly arranged. The logistics were ironed out. Dr. Dobson worked into the wee hours of the next morning, pulling his thoughts together, gathering the facts, and writing his speech.

With more than four thousand people jammed into the courthouse square, a tired yet enthusiastic James Dobson stepped to the microphone and rallied the supporters of Chief Justice Roy Moore. After describing the road that brought them to this moment, he spoke personally and emotionally: "There was a time, when I was younger," he said, "that it stung me to be called a right-winger. There was a time when I didn't want to take the heat. There was a time when I wanted to say what I needed to say, but then tried to keep my head down. I've got to tell you. Those days are over." The crowd roared its approval.

I wish I could say his speech was the catalyst that turned the ship around. Unfortunately, just days later, federal officials wheeled the monument away and pushed it into a dark closet, just feet away from where it once stood.

As a result, critics might consider the trip a failure. I disagree.

You see, Dr. Dobson's trip to Montgomery on August 28, 2003, exemplified the truest form of leadership. Given an opportunity to affect change, he jumped at the chance. He stopped what he was doing, lost himself in the cause, and rolled with circumstances. He didn't send someone in his place—he went himself. Victory was his goal, but the honor of the battle was just as important as the end result. His calendar had him coming home to a day of rest and recuperation in Colorado Springs; instead, he found himself standing under a 100-degree humid and sunny sky. This is who he is. The calendar is merely a suggestion if the Lord has another plan, however late the hour may be.

In our offices, yesterday is history . . . and tomorrow? Mystery! That's because Dr. Dobson doesn't believe in chasing after the plans of man but instead chooses to seek out the will of God. Theoretically, you might expect this in the world of ministry, but practically, it's easier said than done. Thorough planning is a part of any successful venture, but success finds its root in the source of the plan, not simply in the process itself. In other words, God won't bless anything that He hasn't first ordained.

And sometimes, God ordains a circumstance to simply teach us a lesson.

DON'T BE ALARMED

The need for flexibility doesn't always show itself in high drama. Sometimes profound lessons can arise from the simplest of circumstances.

It was a bad way to begin a busy day. With the temperature hovering in the single digits and the roads iced over, I was anxious to get an early start. The typical fifteen-minute drive to the office was looking more like an hour as I peered outside to see our car covered in six inches of freshly fallen Colorado snow.

"Look how pretty!" said Julie, my wife of six months. Gathering my bag, I feigned a smile. With four bald tires that I had been meaning to replace since the summer, I wasn't anxious to drive in the snow, however pretty it may have been.

"Okay, let's go!" I offered, trying to sound upbeat, still fumbling for the keys in a bucket we kept by the door. At the time, Julie was working for Focus on the Family as well and we often commuted together. I found the keys, but I couldn't find the button that disengaged the car locks and turned off the alarm. The contraption had broken off the chain months ago, and we had been carrying it around separately ever since.

Knowing that my wife had used the car the previous evening, I quickly turned to her.

"Did you put the alarm button in your purse?" I asked rather impatiently.

Putting her index finger to her lips and raising her eyes in contemplative fashion, she answered in a halting manner. "Uh, hmmm, I-I-I don't think so" was her uncertain reply.

We scoured the apartment. The precious time that I had been trying to save was quickly slipping away. Finally, Julie remembered where she had left the alarm button.

"Uh-oh," she said.

"What?" I asked.

"I remember now where I left it."

"Where?" I responded, half expecting a happy ending.

"I dropped the alarm in the supermarket parking lot last night while I was loading the groceries in the car."

I shook my head, perplexed.

"You what? You dropped it . . . why didn't you pick it up?" I asked incredulously.

Sheepishly, she said, "I meant to, but I just forgot."

I was speechless—and miffed.

Unable to get into the car, we arranged alternative transportation to work and arrived late. All the way, I played the silent martyr. Unable to grasp how my wife could do what she had done, I was eager to find some sympathy from my coworkers.

Although I didn't find it, I did learn a great lesson of life.

After settling in, I walked into Dr. Dobson's office for a brief meeting. Still stewing from the car incident, I began to share my frustration with him. He listened, nodded, sighed, and ultimately, had a good laugh at my expense.

"Paul," he said, in a bemused and fatherly fashion, his lips pursed together in the form of a sly smile, "you've got to learn something. Those things are going to happen as sure as the sun is going to rise. Get used to it! Laugh at it. Your marriage will be the better for it."

That is just one of the many lessons I've learned from Jim Dobson. Accept your circumstances. Make adjustments accordingly. And roll with it.

It comes down to this: James Dobson strives to run Focus on the Family on the same terms and by the same standards he manages his own life. He is a biblical steward in every sense of the phrase. In everything he does, he seeks to conform to the knowledge and will of God. Anything outside those parameters is like the chaff from wheat: worthless and expendable. His priorities are first filtered through his understanding of God's will, not a personally motivated agenda.

POINTS TO REMEMBER

★ Flexibility should increase in direct proportion to how far we're stretched in a circumstance. Welcome the challenge and reach, even if the goal appears beyond grasp.

★ Adaptability is not a measure of compromise; it's a measure of maturity.

★ If you find yourself irritated while dealing with an unchangeable circumstance, change the one thing you can control: your attitude!

★ Show me someone who can make adjustments while failing and I'll show you someone who is only steps from success.

PRACTICAL PRINCIPLE #2

DECIDE WHAT YOU CARE ABOUT
AND YOU'LL KNOW HOW TO ACT

Do not, for one repulse, forego the
purpose that you resolved to effect.
WILLIAM SHAKESPEARE

His words hung in the air like humidity on a hot summer's day.

Seated across from Dr. James Dobson in a wooden high-back chair, I laid my yellow notepad and black felt-tip pen in my lap. I had come into his office to review an upcoming newsletter commemorating the tragic thirtieth anniversary of *Roe v. Wade*. It was early December, 2002. As was customary, I was prepared to take notes of our discussion.

Instead, I simply sat and listened—and learned a lesson in personal conviction.

Pushing his breakfast of an English muffin and jelly aside, Dr. Dobson turned off FOX News from his television and gazed out across the interstate towards the United States Air Force Academy campus, its buildings silhouetted against the snow-covered mountains and brilliant blue morning sky. Given the seriousness of the topic, his reflective mood did not surprise to me.

I had just been reading some comments from the more militant proabortion crowd and surmised that their rhetoric seemed edgier and shriller than ever. In discussing the horrors of partial-birth abortion, their tone was simply inconceivable to me. I wondered aloud how anyone could entertain the murder of a baby by puncturing its skull with a sharp instrument—all under the guise of personal rights. Dr. Dobson agreed.

"After thirty years," I asked, "don't you ever grow weary of the battle?"

Rubbing his brow, he looked off into the distance before answering. "Paul," he said, his words unfolding slowly, "I want to tell you a story that you may never have heard before."

Clearing his throat, he began. "When I was at the University of Southern California School of Medicine, I was surrounded by people who were in favor of abortion. I was still a young man, having just finished my own graduate work. It was the late 1960s, and the culture was beginning to spin out of control. One of the popular arguments back then was that unwanted and uncared for children were being born into a society unprepared for them, and it would probably be better if they never came into the world in the first place."

His hands were folded on the desktop as he continued, "During that time, I would talk to my father about this, telling him what I heard in some of my circles, and he would get big tears in his eyes and say, 'No, no, no Jimmy. I could never put a politician in office who would do this to an unborn child.' His passion led me back into the Scriptures, and I began to investigate just what the real issues were."

Shifting ever so slightly, his eyes moved from me to the window and the mountains toward the western horizon. "Right about that time," he said, "there was a young woman I was counseling who wanted to have an abortion. I tried to talk her out of it, but"—his words were halting—"I . . . wasn't successful. Of course, although I didn't play a part in the actual abortion, I made it possible for her to do it. I drove her to the hospital. Oh, how I regret that. That was the first, last, and only time I ever facilitated that kind of tragedy."

As he was telling me this story, I could see the tears welling in his eyes. I sat in silence, realizing that I was witnessing the retelling of a remarkably painful—but revealing—personal memory.

"Paul," he concluded, "that's why we're here. To fight for those babies. That's why though we may weary, we never tire. And I will tell you this: I will fight this evil until the day I die."

Molded by memory and convicted by strong personal beliefs, Dr. James Dobson expends little energy debating his course of action. He knows what he cares about, and therefore he knows how to act.

When I first approached Dr. Dobson with my idea for this book, he predictably scoffed at the suggestion. "I have never managed according to the rules of business," he said, "and I'm not a professionally trained businessman. I've always managed according to my instincts and the desire to do what is right."

It is this spirit that lies at the heart of James Dobson and Focus on the Family. It is the hallmark of his management style. He'd rather stand alone for the right reasons than together with a crowd full of wrongheaded people.

But from where does this attitude emanate? Is it merely an emotional reaction or an intellectual response to an academic question? Indeed, those are components of its substance, but they do not serve as its ultimate source.

To fully understand what stirs the soul of Dr. James Dobson, one needs to look no further than the life and mission of Jesus Christ. This is the foundation on which he stands. It is the lodestar of his life. In Jesus, Dr. Dobson finds the source of his strength, the model for his actions, and the purpose of his existence. Without a loving Lord to steer by, anything and everything is ultimately meaningless.

MANAGING ACCORDING TO GOD'S POINT OF VIEW

Dr. Dobson loves to play a game with audiences when he is invited to speak at a convention or a gathering of friends. He asks them the following question: "What was the very first thing that God created when He set out to create the universe?" Naturally, most people go to Genesis. Is it the heavens or the earth? The light or the deep? The answer is actually *wisdom,* as revealed in the eighth chapter of Proverbs, verses 23-25. Here we see wisdom metaphorically speaking in the first person.

> *I have been established from everlasting,*
> *From the beginning, before there was ever an earth.*
> *When there were no depths I was brought forth,*
> *When there were no fountains abounding with water.*
> *Before the mountains were settled,*
> *Before the hills, I was brought forth.* (NKJV)

If Jesus Christ defines us, wisdom sustains us. If wisdom was the first thing ever created, doesn't it make sense that it be a foundational precept of leadership? Nowhere is wisdom more crucial—or more sorely missed—than in the art of leading and managing people. Indeed, wisdom is glorious, it is better than gold (Proverbs 16:16) and it is more powerful than weapons of war (Ecclesiastes 9:18). Simply put, wisdom is seeing things from God's point of view. Wisdom is as important to a true leader as wings are to a bird. Other qualities and characteristics may be more colorful and captivating, but the leader who lacks wisdom is, in reality, no leader at all.

For Dr. James Dobson, wisdom—that is, God's point of view—is the moral foundation of the universe. That universe, he is convinced, has a Boss who has very clear ideas of right and wrong. It doesn't matter much what you or I might think; what matters is what God thinks.

FIRST IMPRESSIONS

On the weekend prior to my first day working in his office, I stopped by Focus on the Family to drop off a box of personal reference books. With reserved excitement, I opened the door of my own office, empty except for a desk, a table, three filing cabinets, two computers, and a phone on the desk.

Dropping the box on the conference table in the corner, I turned on my heels to leave, and as I did so, peered curiously through the inside window of Dr. Dobson's office suite. All was silent as the late-afternoon sun came streaming through his windows. Now authorized to enter as a result of my new position, I thought it might be worthwhile to take a look around.

It was an impressive sight for a man who had spent his entire career working in a cubicle. Two massive windows covered the western wall, providing sweeping views of the Colorado Rockies and, in particular, Pikes Peak. Warmly furnished with two maroon plaid couches, a large square coffee table, and a leather high-back chair, the area evoked a dignified yet comfortable and cozy feel. Dr. Dobson's desk, constructed of dark wood with a glass top, was neat, organized, and positioned squarely in front of floor-to-ceiling built-in oak bookcases. On the other side of the wall behind his desk was his library and personal study. A long, wooden table filled the center of the room with five chairs on either side. Just beyond the library was a door to Dr. Dobson's wife, Shirley's, office. And in an area accessible to both was a small kitchen with a refrigerator, a microwave, and a coffeepot.

Those were some of the first things I saw. But as I stood there, thinking about the responsibilities and opportunities that were now mine to experience, I began noticing items that were more than just functional furniture. These were details that spoke to the priorities of James Dobson.

In the bookcase behind his desk, within arm's length, stood a total of thirty-nine Bibles of varying translations and commentaries. How fitting and proper for a man who sees all things through the prism of Scripture to keep the infallible Word of God so close at hand.

On that same shelf was an original series of books written by Sir Winston Churchill, their covers aged and pages well-worn. An unabashed admirer of the late British prime minister, Dr. Dobson's office was full of Churchill memorabilia. Over one of his couches hung a massive portrait of the man who had rallied his nation in its darkest hour. Considering how often Dr. Dobson finds himself in a lonely battle with long odds, the life of Sir Winston is a suitable source of inspiration.

Over another couch was a much smaller—but much more personal—hand-sketched portrait of his late father, James Dobson Sr. His expression is peaceful and his eyes appear to be gazing downward, assuredly and contently, perhaps in the direction of his son, to whom his unfinished ministry was passed. As a young man, Dr. Dobson's father was an accomplished artist who gave up a potential art career to preach the gospel in varying pastoral positions. As a remembrance of his father's earlier career, there hangs, just above the console floor television, an exquisite rendering of Rembrandt's famous portrait *Jan Six,* painted in his dad's own hand.

On the top of his desk were two photographs—one of his wife, Shirley, and the other a family photo with his daughter, Danae, and son, Ryan. They are his ultimate earthly priorities and the wellspring of great joy and satisfaction.

As I looked around, I saw additional items that spoke subtly to the substance of the man. A framed photo of his late canine companion, Mitzi, sat at eye level on another shelf. Once beaten and malnourished, she had been rescued by the Dobsons from the pound and inevitable death. This type of sensitivity speaks for itself.

Not all of the things I first noticed were poignant or symbolic. Some, like a gumball machine in the corner, were fun and fitting for an office of a child psychologist. On the coffee table between the couches there were numerous toy trucks, cars, puzzles, and books. When parents come in to visit, says Dr. Dobson, children care little about what he has to say. These items keep the child occupied and the parents of sound mind!

As I turned to leave, I was left with this conclusion: These are the things he cares about, and these are the things that define the man I'm about to work for: God's Word; his family, both past and present; the lessons of history and the models of unshakable and unflappable leadership; a proper perspective on life's priorities; and gentleness and compassion for the defenseless.

I arrived home that evening humbled by the prospects of my new job. Sitting on my porch in downtown Colorado Springs, I wrote the following words into a notebook:

SCRIPTURE. FAMILY. HISTORY'S LESSONS.

These are things he thinks about

These are the things he knows

These are the things he prays about

These are the seeds he sows

These are things that matter

These are the things that go fast

These are the things time will scatter

These are the things that will last

THE FUNDAMENTALS

Having served Dr. Dobson for several years now, one thing remains abundantly clear: His actions mirror his convictions, and his convictions mirror his actions. He practices what he preaches.

A private phone number, known only by his family, makes him directly accessible. If Shirley, Danae, or Ryan phone in the middle of a meeting, he will take the call. Family comes first.

Unfortunately, reality suggests that such a commonsense

approach to leadership is not that common. It is very simple, but it seems that the more simple the leadership principle, the more confounded people become. If we would come to terms with what we believe and care about, our course of action would also become clear.

POINTS TO REMEMBER

★ Draw your convictions from the successes and failures of previous experiences and you'll find future decisions far easier to make.

★ Seek godly perspective in all circumstances. Allow God's point of view to shape your goals and outlook in life.

★ When leading others, steer your ship according to standards and values that have stood the test of time. Morality is a nonnegotiable filter through which all decisions must first pass.

★ Prioritize in accordance with a long-term perspective and you'll inevitably discover short-term success.

ASK OTHERS TO GO ONLY WHERE YOU'VE FIRST GONE YOURSELF

*Sincerity is to speak as we think, to do as we
pretend and confess, to perform and make
good what we promise, and really to be what
we would seem and appear to be.*

JOHN TILLOTSON

Like most people, I first met Dr. James Dobson on the radio.

We became fast friends, even though he did most of the talking. Having worked for WOR-AM in New York City, I looked forward to his daily ninety-second commentaries more than any other feature on the radio dial. Juxtaposed with the complexity of midtown Manhattan, his words were simple though the issues of which he spoke were not. Strung together like pickets on a fence, his messages always ran in a straight and logical line. Sometimes they were powerful, often they were poignant, but always they caused me to pause and think.

He struck me as the kind of guy you'd like to have as a neighbor. He was the friend you could sit with on the front porch over a glass of iced tea and talk about matters both big and small. I saw him as the Ward Cleaver of radio—though in my mind, he wasn't just a fuzzy fictional character but instead a real

17

man who rolled up his sleeves and did battle with the real world. Wise, magnanimous, humble. This was the man I thought of whenever I heard him speak.

But could he really be that good? After all, I was basing my estimation of the man on a mere 450 seconds of talk a week. What was he like the remaining 604,350 seconds? Admittedly, I was setting the bar high. It was risky business. This was in the early 1990s, and cynicism and disillusionment were quickly becoming both habit and hobby for the mainstream media establishment. The further the fall the better—and nothing generated more salacious headlines than the depiction of a saint turned sinner. Given my growing appreciation of Dr. Dobson's ministry from only an outside perspective, skeptical acquaintances of mine suggested that disappointment was inevitable. He was a Bible-thumper. A morality maker. I heard it all. Placing your trust in a man was akin to placing a bet on a horse.

Of course, because my admiration was rooted in the teachings he espoused as opposed to the few personal qualities of which I was aware, I wasn't bothered much by the teasing. Simply put, something seemed different about Dr. James Dobson. It wasn't that I thought he was perfect; I knew he was a confessed sinner like me. So I dug deeper. Contacting Focus on the Family directly and visiting my local library, I devoured every bit of information I could find about both Dr. Dobson and the ministry itself. The precepts behind the radio show—the idea that as goes the family, so goes the nation—resonated with me as an idea whose time had come. Having recently graduated from college and with my position in radio, I wondered if God might use me in the ministry of Focus on the Family.

In 1995, a few friends and I traveled west from New York to visit the newly opened Coors Baseball Field in Denver and to catch three games between the Rockies and our hometown club, the Mets. On a Friday afternoon, I convinced the guys to take a drive fifty-five miles south to Colorado Springs and the campus of Focus on the Family. My initial impressions garnered from what I had read and heard were only confirmed after the brief visit. The staff was polite, the buildings were warm and inviting, and the ministry's mission was evident from those we spoke with, from the radio program we heard being recorded, and from the film we saw in the Welcome Center theater.

My buddies joked that the place was a bastion of cleanliness and wholesomeness and that a wayward move on our part would be like a shout in the sanctuary of a church. In fact, on our walk back to our car, we spotted a tilted barrel that seemed to confirm that suspicion. At first glance it appeared to be a garbage can, but we soon discovered that others had made the same mistaken assumption. The barrel was used to hold ice melt, not garbage. Painted across the bottom were the following words: **NO TRASH.** Given our conversation, we laughed at the irony. After all, any organization that endeavored to hold the line on rubbish—literally or figuratively—was a place I thought I'd like to work.

THE THINGS YOU DON'T SEE

Of course, things are not always as they appear. Though we may look closely, we sometimes don't see clearly. When I accepted my position at Focus on the Family, I wanted to know if James Dobson was the same man I had come to know only in my mind. Did his walk match his talk?

Bottom-lining it, I wondered, *Is he the real deal? Does he lead only where he is willing to go himself?*

I quickly discovered that the answer to those questions was yes—but more from his subtle and unseen policies than any deliberate or calculated grand gesture.

In a recent radio broadcast with legendary college basketball coach John Wooden, Dr. Dobson remarked with admiration that humility and sincerity were core characteristics of Coach Wooden's life. The same could be said of James Dobson. A student of God's Word, he considers those qualities to be of utmost importance. The apostle Paul reminded the church at Corinth that we're not to "peddle the word of God for profit." Instead, he taught that "in Christ we speak before God with sincerity" (2 Corinthians 2:17). He warned the Philippians to "do nothing out of selfish ambition or vain conceit, but in humility consider others better than yourselves" (Philippians 2:3). In Proverbs 18:12, we are cautioned that "before his downfall a man's heart is proud, but humility comes before honor."

Humility and sincerity are foundational characteristics in the life of every genuine leader. Unfortunately, especially in the United States, it isn't always easy to be both sincere and humble, at least not at the same time. We tend to fake it till we make it and when we legitimately make it, we often forget how many hands helped us get there. Similarly, our own pride often gets in the way of a good deed. A few years ago, the *Wall Street Journal* captured this conundrum perfectly in its daily *Pepper and Salt* cartoon. Two monastic monks are pictured, replete in their simple robes cinched at the waist by a twisted rope. Says one to the other, "Hey, I figure as long as I'm humble, I might as well flaunt it!"

Suffice it to say, James Dobson is no show-off. If you were to visit the campus of Focus on the Family, you'd see many things, but one thing you'll never see is his name on a building. He doesn't hunger for the trappings of celebrity. If his opinion is needed on the placement of a picture or piece of furniture in a public area, he often waits until evening so as not to disturb tours or interrupt business. He doesn't arrive to work each day with great fanfare but instead enters through a side door in silence. He keeps a low profile considering how high profile a man he is.

WATCH HOW ORDINARY
On the night prior to one of Dr. Dobson's appearances on CNN's *Larry King Live,* I was meeting with several of my colleagues in our public policy division. The discussion turned to

wardrobe. *What color suit had he worn the previous time he was on CNN? What about the tie? Did he wear a white or blue shirt?* Compared with the volumes of research we'd been combing through in preparation, this was a very minor detail, but it's something you think about before your boss appears on national television. In the course of our discussion, someone brought up the subject of his wristwatch. A large, black digital Casio with a calculator panel on the face, the watch always seemed to jump out at the camera as he sat with his hands folded on the desk in front of him. We chuckled. While we knew he wouldn't spend three thousand dollars for a Rolex, we thought he deserved something more elegant than a fifteen-dollar Wal-Mart special, circa 1990. I volunteered to broach the subject with him before leaving for the evening.

I got my chance two hours later. On the way out of our last meeting, we were casually chatting about the next day's schedule.

"By the way, Doctor," I said a bit hesitantly, not wanting him to think I was criticizing his taste, "the guys and I were talking and we wondered if you might want to consider changing watches for tomorrow night's CNN broadcast."

Incredulous, he replied, "Why would I want to do *that*?"

"Well," I answered, "your stature seems to demand a more substantial watch. Maybe something silver or a bit dressier?"

His answer was classic.

"Are you kidding me?" he began, his head shaking off my suggestion. "This is me. This is who I am. *I am Everyman!*"

While his comments contained some humor, they contained quite a bit more, too. Dr. Dobson knows that in God's sight, we are all equal. He understands that money or power mean nothing in terms of our relationship to the Creator. In this way, he truly *is* Everyman.

He drives a five-year-old car, lives in a simple condo, and wears well-tailored but conservative clothing. He regularly eats home-cooked meals, pays for his own lunch, and is fastidiously timely for appointments and personal engagements. At sixty-eight years old, he works, at minimum, approximately sixty hours per week. He doesn't gripe or growl—he simply gets the job done.

A GENUINE SPIRIT

Some time ago, on the morning of one of Dr. Dobson's appearances on *Larry King Live*, a colleague of mine found himself on the phone, ironing out some of the details for that evening's program with a CNN producer. In the midst of the conversation, the network representative happened to ask if Dr. Dobson had the time to talk with another producer who, as a single mom, was having severe disciplinary problems with her four-year-old boy. Might he have some advice for her? My friend assured him that he'd pass the message on, but due to preparations for the show and other commitments, it might be a few days before the boss could call her to discuss the challenges she was currently facing.

The message was relayed to Dr. Dobson as he busily prepared for the live, hour-long grilling that night. By three o'clock that same afternoon, James Dobson was on the phone with the frustrated young mother, oblivious to the pile of briefing papers he still needed to review.

"Oh, we had a wonderful conversation," recalls Dr. Dobson. "She had the very best intentions, but I urged her to get down on the floor with the little guy, go nose to nose with him, and make sure he knew who was boss!"

I was struck by that story, not because of Dr. Dobson's desire to help, but because of the priority to which he assigned the request. At a time when most people would be thinking of themselves—after all, in a matter of hours the world would be watching him on television—James Dobson's thoughts and energies were directed to a mother in desperate need of encouragement and counsel.

DO AS I SAY—DO AS I'VE DONE

Having come out of the newspaper industry, I've had a number of bosses who rarely practiced what they preached. When the first paper I worked for became available via the Internet, those of us on the classified sales team were asked to begin offering our clients the option of posting their advertisement online as well as in the printed paper for an extra five dollars. It seemed like a good deal—until I discovered that every advertisement, regardless of whether or not the client paid the extra fee, was available via the Internet. Alarmed, I questioned my supervisor and was summarily told to pipe down and stop worrying about a measly five bucks! These types of contradictions were common. Please be honest with us, they seemed to say, but let us worry about how honest we are with our customers. Please take just one hour for lunch, but don't be surprised if we take two. It's difficult to respect those leaders who seem to flaunt the very rules they set for their employees.

But James Dobson is different. He never asks you to do something that, if given the opportunity, he wouldn't first do himself.

Just recently, Dr. Dobson was revising and rewriting one of his early best sellers, *The Strong-Willed Child.* The project was a long time in the making, and it came amid dozens of other ministry opportunities each as time sensitive and critical as the next. I was putting in some late hours myself, assisting him with updated research and figures that were relevant to the new manuscript. As one particular week drew to a close, my patience was running thin. After staring at a computer screen for ten hours a day, I was coming home with a nightly headache. In one final Friday night flurry, I completed my work and handed Dr. Dobson his Macintosh laptop, a four hundred–page draft, and a boatload of new material. I was grateful for a two-day break.

My wife and I enjoyed a restful, quiet Saturday. Early

Sunday morning, I logged on to our computer to check e-mail and discovered the following message from my boss:

> Well Paul, it is 12:20 AM—I've been working since 8 AM, and I have had it. Though I'm not thinking straight at this point, it appears that the book is virtually done. Praise the Lord. All that's left that I can recall are the references and a few loose ends.
>
> Hope you're fast asleep. You're a good man, Charlie Brown. Say hello to Julie for us, and have a great Sunday in the Lord.
>
> JCD

This is what you call a perspective check. When you realize that your boss is working sixteen hours on a Saturday, it's a lot easier to give him your absolute best effort the rest of the week. Experience may be the best teacher, but living by example is surely the greatest enforcer of lessons taught.

These long Saturdays, however, are rare. Careful to protect family time, Dr. and Mrs. Dobson often take extended writing trips to such locales as Palm Springs, Boston—even London— to simply get away from the distractions of the office. Dr. Dobson writes for several hours during the day, and then he and Shirley will sightsee, catch a show, or have dinner together.

It's been a good lesson for me, too. Work has its place—but not at the expense of family.

BLITZING THE BELTWAY

On Capitol Hill in Washington, D.C., the name James Dobson is met with either delight or disdain depending upon what side of the issue one comes down on. That's because if Dr. Dobson asks his radio audience to call their senator, congressperson, or president to express an opinion on a particular piece of legislation, they do just that.

The congressional switchboards have sometimes been jammed for hours following Focus on the Family broadcasts. At times, officials have told us, the sheer volume of calls has caused technical meltdowns that required entire computer phone systems to be rebooted.

Why do people listen to him? Why do they call? First, they call because they care passionately about the issue. Second (and almost as important) they call because they respect and trust the man who asked them to call. They call because they know that Dr. Dobson has first called himself.

BOILING IT ALL DOWN

If you were to ask me if Dr. James Dobson is a difficult man to work for, I'd tell you yes. He stretches his employees. He challenges them. His persistence sometimes even tries their patience. Yet because he possesses both a spirit of sincerity and one of humility, it's easy to respond enthusiastically to his requests. In summation, here is how he captures the essence of each trait:

Sincerity: When he speaks, you not only believe what he says, you believe he believes it too. His emotion is never feigned or phony. He will never invest energy in a cause that he doesn't consider worthy of his attention.

Humility: He is not arrogant. He lives simply and speaks softly. He carries his own weight. He never tries to be better than someone else, but instead only tries to better himself by learning from others.

These two traits yield results even more valuable in the life of a leader and the lives of those under his supervision: reliability and predictability. When the charge is given, no one needs to waste time debating the merits or motivation behind the task at hand.

Dr. Dobson's go-where-I've-gone leadership style is not a

new one. He takes his cues from the ultimate Leader: Jesus Christ. For the past fifty years, radio commentator Paul Harvey has offered what he calls "the world's shortest sermon" every Easter weekend. It consists of one sentence:

> Jesus lived the good life in a wicked world to show us that it could be done, and he died and rose again to show us that we could do that, too.[1]

Two thousand years later, our model for living is still the life of Jesus Christ. Though we repeatedly fall short, we nonetheless struggle to emulate His example. The Savior never asks us to do anything that He hasn't first done Himself.

POINTS TO REMEMBER

★ To the world, our actions scream but our words often only whisper. Don't simply point in the direction you're looking to lead; show the way by your walk as well as by the tone of your talk.

★ Over time, sincerity yields legitimacy, and legitimacy yields influence.

★ Don't ask anyone to go where you're not willing to first go yourself.

GOOD WILL IS THE FIRST LAW
OF GOOD BUSINESS

What I gave I have, what I spent I had;
and what I left is lost.
ROBERT OF DONCASTER

Generosity is like a bolt of lightning out of a clear, blue sky. It arrives without warning. It is random and unpredictable. As quickly as it comes, it goes, and its effects can linger long after it touches its target.

This is a story of one of those times.

As a United Airlines ticket counter agent at the Colorado Springs Airport, Bonnie Haskell first got to know Dr. James Dobson in the early 1990s when Focus on the Family was finalizing its move from Pomona, California, to its current location. Their friendship grew as fast as any relationship could through a series of five-minute exchanges. While all were pleasant, one, in particular, stands out in Bonnie's memory.

"Hello, Bonnie! How're you doing? What's new?" asked Dr. Dobson as he arrived at the counter to check in before heading back to California. Despite her smile, her usual cheerful disposition seemed to be missing.

"Oh, I'm doing great," answered Bonnie, "but I have this

friend who has been on my mind lately, and she's really having a tough time."

Without hesitation, Dr. Dobson put down his briefcase, folded his hands on the counter, and said with great empathy, "Do you have a moment to tell me about it?"

She did. The details of that conversation have been lost in the last ten years, but the rest of the story has not.

Bonnie still recalls how Dr. Dobson stood, his eyes focused on hers—not on his watch—and patiently listened. She doesn't remember what kind of advice he offered. She just knows that he listened.

About three days later, the United Airlines mail courier handed her an envelope just as her shift was ending. It contained a letter that read as follows:

> Greetings, Bonnie. Thank you for taking the time to talk earlier this week. Please cash the enclosed check and pass its proceeds on to your friend. I hope it helps in some small way.
>
> GOD'S BLESSINGS,
> *Jim Dobson*

Imagine sending a check to a woman you've never met because of a two-minute conversation with another woman you barely know. That's generosity.

Among those who know him, Dr. Dobson is viewed as a tough-minded man with a soft spot for those in need. Much, if not most, of his giving happens behind closed doors. In the hallways of Focus on the Family, it is sometimes whispered about but never openly discussed. You will never see him on a stage handing over one of those large ceremonial checks for his own personal aggrandizement. He'll never bring up his own charitable giving in conversation. Instead, he gives in the privacy of his office or in a one-on-one discussion. Few people are aware that he's been Focus on the Family's largest donor over the course of the last twenty-seven years. He donates all the royalties from his books distributed via our bookstore or radio offers to Focus.

ULTRASENSITIVE

In January of 2004, at Focus on the Family's monthly chapel service, those in attendance viewed a live ultrasound of Wendy and Chris Jeub's preborn baby. (Chris worked in our Internet department.) In a private room backstage, a portable ultrasound machine had been brought in, and the Jeubs gave permission for the video of the exam to be broadcast to the large screens hanging in the chapel. It was an emotional presentation as the Jeubs were informed for the first time that in just a few short months, a boy would be joining their family.

The 1,500 people in the audience roared their congratulations. (I'm happy to report that Josiah James was born into the world on May 24, 2004, weighing in at a healthy eight pounds!)

Following the service, the Rev. H. B. London, the chapel facilitator, spoke with the Jeub family and was surprised to discover that in addition to their preborn child, the family consisted of *ten* other children, ranging in age from twenty months to twenty years old. What amazed H. B. more than the size of the family, though, was the fact that they were able to get by on Chris's modest salary.

Given the logistical issues of getting ten children to sit down for a meal all at the same time, H. B. asked one of the younger girls if they ate breakfast together as a family.

"Of course!" came the reply.

"What did you eat this morning?" he asked.

"Ummmm . . . a muffin!" she responded.

"A muffin?" countered H. B. in a playful tone. "Don't you like cereal?"

Chris's reply nearly broke his heart.

"Well," said Chris, "cereal is a bit too expensive—things like cinnamon toast seem to go a lot further!"

A few days later, wind of this conversation reached Dr. Dobson, who invited Chris up to the executive wing. As he entered, Chris mentioned how honored he was to be in the chairman's office. "Are you kidding?" shot back James Dobson. "I'm the one who's impressed with you! Feeding, caring for, and homeschooling a family of that size is impressive. You're to be commended."

As their thirty-minute conversation wound down, Dr. Dobson asked Chris a question.

"I don't want to offend you, Chris," he began, "but when H. B. told me how you and your family have to steer clear of cereal because of the cost, I thought about all of this food we've recently received as Christmas gifts and wondered if you might want some of it. It's just the two of us at home," he said, "and there's no way we could possibly eat all of this ourselves. I'm sure you can put some turkey and smoked salmon to good use." Chris gratefully accepted. The box was overflowing. Then Dr. Dobson handed him two envelopes and simply said, "Here's something to help with groceries and another that I hope you spend on just you and your wife." Chris again thanked him profusely. "Please don't thank me," said Dr. Dobson. "Thank God."

On another occasion, Focus on the Family employee Mike Benzie recalls a taxi ride he took with Dr. Dobson during which the cabbie shared a personal struggle in his marriage and asked for advice. At the end of the ride, James Dobson reached into his wallet, pulled out some money and said, "Please take your wife to dinner." These are the habits of a quiet giver, a man whose spirit of generosity is best captured when the rest of the world is looking the other way.

MOTIVATING FACTORS

These stories are not offered to show you how great a guy James Dobson is. His giving isn't mandated by committee or done with the hope of making himself—or even Focus on the Family—look good. Dr. Dobson's good will has nothing to do with the business of James Dobson; it has *everything* to do with the business of Jesus Christ. It's about ministry, not money. It's about salvation, not personal success.

However, Scripture pulls no punches about the benefits that come to a generous and grateful giver. In Psalm 112:5, we read that "all goes well for those who are generous, who lend freely and conduct their business fairly" (NLT). In Proverbs, the Lord assures us that "the generous prosper and are satisfied; those who refresh others will themselves be refreshed" (Proverbs 11:25, NLT). The apostle Paul used a wonderful metaphorical reminder when he wrote to the church at Corinth: "A farmer who plants only a few seeds will get a small crop. But the one who plants generously will get a generous crop" (2 Corinthians 9:6, NLT).

When I look at the life of Dr. Dobson, I see the truths of Scripture. The Lord has sustained him through illness, blessed him with a creative mind, and granted him energy far in excess of most people his age. His days are full of purpose, and his personal life is overflowing with people he loves and who love him in return. I believe these are but a few of the gifts granted to this man who lives according to God's Word.

TIME AND TALENT

Our treasure is hardly the only means by which to express generosity and good will. The Greek philosopher Theophrastus, the favorite pupil and successor of Aristotle, suggested that "time is the most valuable thing a man can spend." Benjamin Franklin remarked that "time is money." More cynically yet comically, Will Rogers once opined that "half our life is spent trying to find something to do with the time we have rushed through life trying to save." However you make use of your time, there's one thing that most of us can agree on: We wish we had more of it.

Dr. Dobson is no exception. But it's also something that he readily gives away to those who ask.

Gary Lydic, who's been working for Focus on the Family for more than twenty years, remembers a trip he took with Dr. Dobson back in 1988 to attend a funeral.

Allow me to share Gary's memory in his own words:

It was an emotional and hectic day and we were scrambling to catch our flight. We didn't have any time to spare. If we missed the flight to Detroit, we'd miss the funeral. We made our way through security and were hustling and bustling to the gate. I was carrying less and soon found myself a few steps in front of Jim. A minute later, I looked back—no Dr. Dobson. I began to panic. Where did he go? We were going to miss the plane. Then, out of the corner of my eye, I saw him sitting down, listening to a woman who had apparently recognized him and hoped a word or two would help her with a problem. He was a picture of patience. Even if it meant missing that flight— which we didn't—he was going to give that woman the only thing she wanted: his time. Dr. Dobson will give his time to anyone, anywhere.

During a recent discussion with a group of Focus staff members, an employee apologized to Dr. Dobson for interrupting his breakfast a few months back at a local hotel. This man's wife, excited to see the Dobsons just a table away, had approached them and chatted for a few minutes. "You probably get tired of people butting in to your private time, don't you?" asked the staff member.

"Oh my goodness, no," replied Dr. Dobson. "I've never objected to people saying hello. If I did, I shouldn't be doing what I'm doing. Imagine, people listen to our radio program and read my books, and I can't find the time to say hello? Never!"

LENDING A HELPING HAND

In addition to the giving of our treasure and time, the sharing of our talents is another way to spread good will. Scripture contains a blueprint for the attitude and impetus that should accompany our gift. We're warned not to store up earthly treasure (Matthew 6:19; Luke 12:21, 33) but instead to spend on things of eternal value.

Many requests of varying nature come through our office. Groups often ask Dr. Dobson to speak at their fund-raising events. Families ask for taped video greetings for fiftieth wedding anniversary celebrations. Television, radio, and print media call regularly—all seeking a comment or perspective on an issue. Books are sent in for an inscription. Dr. Dobson receives dinner invitations, business proposals—even date requests for his children! No matter the request—with the exception of the romance proffers for Danae and Ryan—Dr. Dobson prayerfully considers every appeal. There are two things he cannot do, however. The first is endorse books and write forewords. Time simply does not permit it and the board of directors has issued a directive prohibiting Dr. Dobson from doing it. Second, he is rarely able to travel and speak. The pressures of daily radio, television, and other activities make it impossible for him to be gone unless absolutely necessary.

As mentioned earlier, the proceeds from all of Dr. Dobson's books sold through Focus on the Family are donated directly to the ministry. This contribution is significant. As an example, the best seller *When God Doesn't Make Sense* has generated well over three million dollars since publication and has helped fund countless programs designed to strengthen the family.

James Dobson understands that nothing he owns is really his; all that he has belongs to God. This conviction can be traced all the way back to his college years.

H. B. London is Focus on the Family's vice president of Ministry Outreach/Pastoral Ministries. A pastor for thirty-one years, the Reverend London has a real heart for the needs and concerns of the clergy. He is also a cousin of Dr. Dobson and professes a long and storied history of giving him a hard time while they were growing up. Of course, as any man worth his salt would, Dr. Dobson could also give it right back!

During their freshman year of college, H. B. London recalls how Dr. Dobson became concerned that his cousin wasn't tithing 10 percent of his college allowance to the local church. "Granted, I was a real screwup," says H. B., "but he was really bothered by that. He thought I was in grave spiritual danger!" When man-to-man discussions didn't change things, a concerned Jim Dobson wrote a respectful but pointed note to H. B.'s mother (Jim's aunt), expressing his concerns. "That was typical of Jim," says H. B., now laughing as he remembers the story. "He took those kinds of things seriously!"

POINTS TO REMEMBER

★ God owns it all—none of our blessings are ours to keep. All gifts are ours to give. We are commanded to give freely and hold all things with an open hand.

★ The adulation of man is meaningless. We are not to give in exchange for what we may get in return. It matters not whether our generosity is ever acknowledged; what matters is that our generosity is received.

★ We need to think more of the things of heaven and less of the things of earth.

PRACTICAL PRINCIPLE #5

THAT WHICH IS NOT TRACKED IS NOT DONE

The art of communication is the
language of leadership.
JAMES HUMES

In 1616, King James I, while corresponding with Sir George More, unknowingly coined a popular cliché when he wrote, "I desire not that ye should trouble me with an answer, if it is no end; and no news is better than evil news."[2]

Is it true? Is no news good news?

In the aftermath of the terrorist attacks of 9/11, we all breathed great sighs of relief when we turned on the television or radio to find regularly scheduled programming. The absence of "news" meant one thing: Nothing else bad had happened. No more hijacked airliners, no more skyscrapers reduced to rubble, no more innocent blood shed in the streets of America.

Indeed, in the days following September 11, 2001, no news *was* good news. But is that always the case?

My work with Dr. Dobson began just as he was putting the finishing touches on his runaway best seller *Bringing Up Boys*. On my very first day in the office, he asked me to chase down some final statistics and secure some last-minute permissions for material he was quoting in the new book. Eager to please and anxious to begin, I marched out of his office and went to work. For the next few days, I mined the manuscript with a fine-tooth comb, dug through research books and files, perused Web pages, made phone calls, and sent dozens of faxes and e-mails seeking answers and information. With the exception of two stubborn permission requests that still had not been returned, I accomplished what I had set out to do. As the week drew to a close, I reported back my findings.

"Great job!" said Dr. Dobson. "But please keep on those two outstanding permissions. We need them."

I assured him that I would—and I did. But the results were slow in coming. Many of my e-mails went unanswered, my phone calls weren't returned, and when contact was made, those with the authority to finalize the request were invariably on vacation or otherwise detained. It was frustrating, but it was part of the job and normal for the business.

In the meantime, Dr. Dobson left for vacation. Although he was out of the office, we still spoke on a regular basis. The topics were varied and driven by the news of the day or upcoming broadcasts, media appearances, or other writing projects. Having not resolved the permissions issue yet, I never brought it up and neither did he.

Until about his second week out of the office.

On this particular day, he had called while taking his daily one-hour walk, this time on the outskirts of Central Park in New York City. In the bustle of midtown Manhattan—the car horns, the screeching tires, and the crush of commuters—the call was wrapping up, and just as I glanced down at my yellow legal pad, filled with questions to be answered and tasks to do, Dr. Dobson began thinking out loud.

"There is something else," he said, his voice trailing off. "I thought of it before. There was something I've been waiting on an answer from you for."

Furiously flipping through my planner, I was at a loss for what he was referring to.

"Oh yes!" he said. "What have you found out about those two permission requests we need for the book?"

Relieved that I had not forgotten to do something he asked, I began explaining how tedious the process had been.

Empathizing, he replied, "I understand, but you have to stay on them. You're asking them to do you a favor; the burden rests on you, not them."

I agreed, reiterating that I had spent the last two weeks calling, faxing, and e-mailing.

"I don't doubt it," he said, "but in the future, let me know what's going on. If you run up against a wall, I might be able to suggest a way over or around it. You should keep me informed."

"Yes, sir," I replied, "but I didn't want to bother you with an unresolved issue."

"Paul," he offered, taking on that tone that's more counselor than caustic, "you've only been in our office for a few weeks, so let me tell you something that's very important for you to remember. If you can remember this, we'll work well together."

As Ross Perot said to the American people in 1992, I was "all ears."

"This place (Focus on the Family) is like Los Angeles International Airport," he said. "On any given day, there are hundreds of planes in the sky over LAX. Even though not every one of them is going to land at the exact same time, the air-traffic controllers need to know about them. They need to know where they are in the sky and what time they can be expected to land. Do you see the parallel? On any given day, there are easily a hundred different issues floating over my desk. I know they can't—and won't—land all at once, but I at least need to know where they are up there. That's where you come in. You're the controller of the issue and you need to let me know of your progress. I have said this before and I'll continue to say it: That which is not tracked is not done."

I had never heard of an office being compared to an airport, but given the ninety different departments at Focus, it made good sense. Imagine how chaotic your local airport might be if no one reported the progress and the status of the planes in the sky? How many needless hours would be wasted waiting for a flight that had been delayed or even canceled? It also helped to explain why in my previous jobs projects often met with one of two fates: They were either halfheartedly completed—but missed hitting the intended target in the process—or they slowly faded away and were forgotten, having never been quite finalized or discussed since the assignment was first given.

That's because if something isn't tracked, it often never gets done.

HOT PENDINGS

To stay on top of the many issues that encircled Focus on the Family while he was president, Dr. Dobson implemented a simple process that he called the *hot pending system*. In short, it was an internal system designed to monitor correspondence, questions, or requests that came out of his office.

If there was a perceived problem, whether with a process, a person, or any other administrative issue, the assignment was boiled down to a question, laid out in a one-page memo, dated, and assigned a deadline for response. If an answer wasn't possible within the time frame allotted, an extension was granted. That's because more important than a deadline was an accurate answer.

These hot pendings were expected to receive top priority among the staff. That's because many of the issues were related to concerns deemed critical to James Dobson's standards of business. For example, why did it take two weeks for the couple struggling to hold their marriage together to receive a book or tape they requested? Or why didn't our radio listeners in Lafayette, Louisiana, hear the special broadcast yesterday? In most cases, the hot pending inquiry led to an answer and, ultimately, a more efficient process that served the constituent in a manner more pleasing to God.

The system has worked effectively for three main reasons:

1. Complex issues are reduced to simple, understandable questions. Dr. Dobson knows that issues are often lost in debate and discussion. When a problem is posed in the form of a question, a practical solution is more likely to be found.
2. The recipient is asked to answer both succinctly and accurately in a timely manner. Any temptation to respond with a colorful bar graph or pie chart is discouraged. Questions are best answered with answers, not more questions.
3. The system helps employees to manage one of our most vexing temptations: the desire to avoid personal accountability. We all wish we could operate on our own personal timetable. We want to be our own boss and decide for ourselves when—and even if—something gets done. If we make a mistake, we'd like it to be overlooked, or if an assignment gets too arduous, we might wish it be forgotten. The hot pending system forces us to keep that temptation in check because the assignment is recorded and multiple people are awaiting an answer. Simply put, no one is an island. Everything we do, or don't do, for that matter, affects someone else in ways both large and small.

FRIEND OR FOE?

Is the hot pending system popular within the rank and file? Probably not, because it holds every staff member to a high level of accountability, just like videos of NFL games provide incredible accountability for the players. The coach can stop the tape at any moment and say, "You blocked that linebacker about six inches too high, which is why he slid around you. If you'd stay lower you would be more explosive." Most corporate leaders know about the major decisions and maneuvers being made daily by their managers. But they have little information about how the details were handled. Perhaps it has to be that way, but progressive coaches in sports will tell you that winning and losing is produced by the little things—the fundamentals. It's there that success or failure is determined. The hot pending system tells the boss immediately how the "blocks and tackling" is going. In Dr. Dobson's case, it allowed him to critique the entire organization from day to day, noting how quickly letters were being answered and how carefully money was being spent. Obviously, the scrutiny made some staffers uncomfortable, but it also made them more effective.

Recently, a longtime friend of Focus on the Family came by for a visit with Dr. Dobson and a few other members of the ministry. In the course of conversation, he remarked to a new member of the staff his desire to contribute a sizable sum of money. Having come to this generous decision rather spontaneously, he only had a credit card and wondered if he might use that in lieu of a check. "Certainly," said the staff member, "the bookstore is equipped to handle such a donation. They are open until 5:30 this evening." With a handshake and a heartfelt thank-you, the staff member said good-bye and left the gentleman in the lobby of the administration building.

The story of this exchange found its way to Dr. Dobson. He was mortified. "That's not the way we treat people," he said. "That staff member should have escorted him over to the bookstore or, at the very least, asked him if he might otherwise assist him. Please find out who he spoke with and why that happened."

The hot pending system was activated. I was asked to make

a few phone calls, and based upon my findings, the employee was identified and the question was asked. Within twenty-four hours, Dr. Dobson received an answer. As it turned out, the individual was new to Focus on the Family. He quickly learned of his oversight. Though embarrassing, it turned into a very teachable moment for the entire department. The employee who unknowingly made the error was given an opportunity to talk with and apologize to the donor. To this day, they're good friends, thanks in part to a system designed to track the goings and comings of an ordinary day.

While the staff may not enjoy their mistakes being highlighted or the burden of another assignment, they realize that this system can improve the day-to-day operations at Focus on the Family. Most importantly, they see that hot pendings often lead to better service for friends of the ministry.

The hot pending system forces people to work for answers to questions and for solutions to problems. It forces the employee to confront and tackle the tough issues rather than avoiding or downright ignoring them. By staying on top of things, the leader is less likely to get buried by them in the first place.

That which gets tracked gets done!

POINTS TO REMEMBER

★ Communication is a vital component of most jobs, even if you're solely responsible for the completion of the task. Very few people operate in total isolation.

★ Keep the communication simple, but keep it regular and keep it coming.

★ If you make the effort to give an assignment, take the time to check on the progress of the job.

WHERE THERE'S SMOKE, THERE'S FIRE

God never gives us discernment in order that
we may criticize, but that we may intercede.
OSWALD CHAMBERS

H. B. London tells the story of how he struggled with his decision to come work at Focus on the Family.

As first cousins, Jim Dobson and H. B. London (both only children) grew up more like brothers than extended relatives. While H. B. felt the Lord calling him to Colorado Springs, he was concerned that familiarity might breed contempt. He didn't want to do anything to jeopardize the close-knit relations both families enjoyed.

"Quite frankly," he told me recently, "we were concerned that we'd kill each other! I love him, but I wasn't sure I would love working with him." Their respective wives, Shirley and Beverly, shared his apprehension. Before making the decision, the two couples decided to meet over dinner and shake things out.

As H. B. recalls, the Dobsons were a bit delayed the evening of the meal. Upon their arrival, Dr. Dobson apologized and explained why they were late.

"I'm sorry to keep you waiting," he began, "but I was busy trying to decide just how we're going to work this out, what with us being family and such good friends to boot." He paused.

Clasping his hands together, he said exuberantly, "But, I've figured it out! The problem is solved."

H. B. was startled to hear that Dr. Dobson had come to such a quick decision over a matter of such concern, especially since the whole point of the dinner had been to talk things out together. Nonetheless, always knowing Jim Dobson to be a fair guy, he remembers being elated with the prospect of a workable solution.

"What have you decided?" asked H. B.

Shaking his head in confident satisfaction, Dr. Dobson responded, "It's real simple, H. I'm the boss. And you're not!"

Of course, that wasn't the end of the discussion. Dr. Dobson regularly seeks the counsel and input of other individuals.

To this day, though, H. B. laughs heartily remembering that evening. Jesting aside, James Dobson is not some sort of dictator who makes decisions void of reason or on the basis of personal ego. Yet, at the same time, his methods of discernment and decision-making are unique in a culture where common sense isn't very common at all.

INVISIBLE INSTINCTS

When it comes to making decisions, most of us tend to rely more on what we see as opposed to what we don't. Taking something at face value is another way of saying that we believe and trust what we see. We also trust what we hear. We have confidence that things really are as they appear at first glance. Unfortunately, this is the basis for how most of us get things done and the measure by which we test the value and worth of a circumstance or situation. We think it's a matter of logical reasoning, when in fact, we're actually drawing conclusions before having all the facts.

It's been my observation that Dr. James Dobson doesn't

operate like this. While he does depend on the obvious, he pays as much attention to what is missing as to what is there. In day-to-day management, he will often look for what *isn't* said, what *isn't* done, and what *isn't* seen. For example, "Why didn't you mention the reason the mailing was late? Was it human error or was it for reasons beyond your control?" Or, "Why didn't that report contain a comparative analysis of year-over-year results? Could it be that the results, when taken in context, aren't as flattering as they now appear?" Or, "Why haven't I seen any draft of that letter yet? Are you falling behind in your work—or is it simply an oversight on your part?"

I've also marveled at Dr. Dobson's ability to read between the lines of popularly touted research, which is very often spun in order to promote a particular ideological position. For example, it's been widely reported for decades that half of all marriages in the United States end in divorce. Is this true? My boss has told me that it isn't, and with some digging into the facts, it's easy to see why the figure is inaccurate. According to Dr. Dobson, people make the mistake of comparing the number of marriages each year with the number of divorces in the same time frame. Let's say there were two hundred marriages and one hundred divorces in a given county over the course of a year. Quick math suggests that the divorce rate is 50 percent, right? Wrong. These statistics fail to take into account the number of marriages that already exist in the county. Based upon the available data, pollsters suggest that the divorce figure could be anywhere between 5 percent and 24 percent—not 50 percent! With a discerning and inquisitive mind, James Dobson sees what most people miss.

Are these the habits of a cynic? No. Are they the ruminations of a skeptic? Perhaps. However, the skepticism is a healthy and well-founded quality tested more in the fires of experience than in the smoldering soup of suspicion. Inquisitive by nature, Dr. Dobson's tendency is to ask questions. Always interested in the details, he loves to gather the facts behind a story, because he knows that undisclosed facts can often explain what an initial read of the conclusion might miss.

With a Ph.D. in child development, he's also very familiar with some of the more challenging habits of human nature. He knows that when it comes to workplace communication, people are more likely to conceal the negative and reveal the positive. This is a big problem because the successful leader must hear both the good *and* the bad—and therein lies a significant challenge and a vexing paradox of management. Many dutiful employees sugarcoat the bad news thinking that the sugar will turn the sour sweet. In reality, the sugar only masks the problem, often making a bad situation much worse. The truth of the matter is this: When we deliberately try to make ourselves or a situation look good when it's undeserved, we more often than not make everyone else—including ourselves—look bad.

By asking questions, Dr. Dobson deliberately facilitates open and direct communication. "Give it to me straight" is a phrase I've heard in our offices on numerous occasions. It's a disarming manner, because people are encouraged to lay the facts before him—and let him draw his own conclusions. It encourages a genuine exchange as opposed to a filtered report that fails to relay the necessary news.

Dr. Dobson doesn't just look for people who will make him look good; instead, he looks for those who will do good work.

SMOKE DETECTOR

Despite a significant amount of verbal communication, our offices are often awash in paper memos. Dr. Dobson's briefcase, which he takes home with him each weekend, is literally a *suitcase* on wheels. (Anyone who's predicting the emergence of a paperless society has obviously never been in the office of our chairman!)

As he makes his way through his correspondence, Dr. Dobson has a habit of communicating his thoughts back to the author of the memo by writing comments in the margin. He asks and answers questions, declines and accepts invitations, and simply acknowledges receipt of news. Some of his directives are pointed; others are benign. Like my first "Gadzooks!" memo mentioned earlier, he has a knack for relaying a significant amount of information with only a few handwritten words. How he writes the message—the size of the print, the punctuation, the use of the underline—is sometimes as telling as what the message itself says.

It should be noted, though, that his style, however pointed it may be, is always gracious and respectful. While admonishing me for my mistake of sending duplicate letters during my first year of work, it wasn't lost on me that he concluded with the sentence: "*Please* be more careful." Pointed—but polite!

When it comes to ferreting out a potential problem and communicating it back to the employee responsible for handling it, James Dobson's direct discernment is probably no better illustrated than with the use of this phrase: *I smell smoke!*

Smoke is another word for "trouble," or a sign of a standard that may have slipped. It may come after Dr. Dobson receives a note from a constituent whose need was not met, or maybe it's in response to a budget allocation that seems to be either too thin or too generous. The smell of smoke doesn't mean someone's in trouble—it simply means that something might be amiss and that he's determined to get to the bottom of it.

FIRE PREVENTION

It could be said that James Dobson started Focus on the Family back in 1977 for the simple reason that he smelled smoke in the air of America. Marriages were crumbling. Children were struggling. The family was falling apart. While most experts saw things unfolding in nothing more than an inevitable cultural continuum, Dr. Dobson believed otherwise. If nothing was done, he surmised, nothing would improve.

Indeed, James Dobson has been like a signalman in the mountains waving a flag to warn of disaster lurking in the distance. In the 1970s, he saw abortion as the slippery slope to greater evil. The "culture of death" that Pope John Paul II has lamented has direct links to this coarsening of human life. The acceptance of partial-birth abortion, cloning, and euthanasia is an outgrowth of the ill-directed Supreme Court decision of 1973. You see, Dr. Dobson has long seen what so many refuse to acknowledge: When it comes to evil or even old-fashioned bad judgment, there is a logical progression of trouble if the problem is not addressed and rectified before things get out of hand.

Or, on a lighter note, in the words of the lovable Barney Fife, when trouble strikes, you've got to "nip it—nip it in the bud!" This is why Dr. Dobson goes for the water when the smell of smoke hits the air.

THE SOURCE

Dr. James Dobson is neither a seer nor prophet, but rather a man who bases his discernment in the inerrant teachings of Scripture. It doesn't matter so much what Dr. Dobson thinks; it only matters what God has to say about the subject. Like blueprints to a builder, Dr. Dobson uses God's Word as his mode of measure.

His ability to smell smoke in the midst of a seemingly clear sky is not some sort of spooky sixth sense. Rather, it is the exercise of *good* sense and the habit of seeing all issues and circumstances through a biblical point of view.

THE PULSE

While Scripture remains his ultimate reference point, it could be said that Dr. Dobson is a man who also manages by feel.

(This may surprise some people, especially those who often criticize conservatives for being heartless and void of emotion!)

Each day he receives a "pulse report" summarizing what types of calls, questions, and comments are coming in from across America in response to his daily radio broadcast. He reads a daily summary of the mail. If he's in a restaurant downtown, he'll talk with people who approach him, and he's not afraid to ask them what they're thinking.

By talking directly to the people who are listening to him on the radio, he's able to keep his finger on the pulse of his constituency and therefore is able to sense when something is amiss.

SMOKE?

Focus on the Family's director of employment David Bervig tells the story of how one local applicant set off Dr. Dobson's smoke alarm in the middle of a weekend meal. While standing in line at a Furr's Cafeteria in Colorado Springs, a gentleman told Dr. Dobson that he had been waiting weeks for an answer to a job application. "Is this the way you treat applicants?" queried the frustrated man. Dr. Dobson apologized, took his name, and promised he'd look into it.

A note from the chairman's office arrived in Human Resources first thing on Monday morning. A brief description of the encounter was included with the general question, "What happened?" Contained within the message were the infamous three words: *I smell smoke!*

An investigation revealed that the applicant *had* been contacted and informed that he didn't meet the qualifications for the position. Consequently, however, he had submitted additional applications for other jobs and the system had yet to catch up with his inquiries. The investigation resulted in a revision of the application process. As it stands today, any pending applicant to Focus on the Family is contacted every ten days until he or she is hired or turned down for the job in question. If people take the time to apply to Focus on the Family, we take the time to respect them in return. These are some of the good things that can happen when James Dobson smells smoke.

FIRE!

In the early days of Focus on the Family, back when it was less than half its current size, Dr. Dobson reviewed every expense that the ministry incurred. It didn't matter if it was as minor as a meal or as major as a mail-sorting machine. He wanted to see it because he wanted to be sure that every donated dollar was wisely spent. He reveled in the detail. It was a smooth process.

Today, thanks to a diligent and responsible staff, Dr. Dobson rarely has to worry about submitted expenses, but when he does, feathers can really fly.

First, some quick background information to help put this next story in context:

With constituents spread from coast to coast, Focus on the Family has several staff members whose main responsibility it is to travel around the country on behalf of Dr. Dobson. They hold meetings known as "updates," during which time they solicit input, entertain questions, and share the latest news regarding Focus on the Family. They also track down and thank the many people who have donated so generously. Given the varying needs they encounter, it is often a time of prayer and fellowship. Other times, it's pure and simple fun.

On one of these occasions, a Focus on the Family representative was invited by a constituent to play a round of golf at his private club. While the rep had the time, he didn't have any clubs. "Not a problem!" assured his new friend. "I have two sets in my trunk. You can use one of them."

When they arrived at the course, the rep was told he couldn't play unless he wore golf spikes. He only had street shoes. "Not a problem!" replied his companion. "Just go on into the pro shop and buy a pair." Not wanting to disappoint or insult his friend, the rep did as he suggested. It was a marvelous day of golf, so marvelous in fact that at the end of the round, this friend of Focus on the Family presented the rep with a check for a staggering $50,000.

When Dr. Dobson was reviewing this employee's expense account, he noticed a reimbursement request for a seventy-five-dollar pair of golf shoes. He didn't sign, but instead wrote beside it, "Gadzooks! I smell smoke. Explain!"

The representative tried to justify the expense by pointing out how little choice he had and the fact that the generosity of the donation more than paid for the shoes in question. Dr. Dobson would hear nothing of it. The end did not justify the means. Sacrificial giving was to pay for a pair of golf shoes? Unacceptable! Unthinkable! A reimbursement of this nature may be common in many successful for-profit companies across the country, but because Focus on the Family is a nonprofit Christian ministry, Dr. Dobson just couldn't approve the reimbursement. Maybe he felt that the employee could have suggested another activity rather than purchase a shiny new pair of shoes. In any event, the employee now had a new pair of golf spikes for his personal use, and having the employee pay for them seemed like the right thing to do.

SENSING BETRAYAL

More recently, Dr. Dobson's intuition helped stave off potential legislative disaster. In November of 2002, the Republican-controlled Congress was on the verge of passing historic bankruptcy reform legislation. It was a good bill, but at the last moment New York Senator Chuck Schumer added a completely unrelated proabortion amendment. (Senator Schumer's amendment singled out abortion protestors as the lone group banned from declaring personal bankruptcy if hit with a lawsuit pertaining to a demonstration.) Given the fact that the Republicans had received more than $45 million of lobbying money from the credit card industry, the pressure for passage was intense.

When reports of this new amendment broke, Dr. Dobson phoned Texas representative Tom DeLay and urged him to vote against it. Though Dr. Dobson recalls him being "sympathetic" to his plea, he sensed that politics were about to trump principle. Simply put, he smelled smoke. On his radio program he urged his listeners to take action. Here is how he described the response in his monthly letter to our constituents:

> *Angry calls flooded into congressional offices by the thousands, and Republicans began to see the light. Ultimately, enough of them teamed with the Democrats to defeat the bill—over the impassioned objection of the Republican leadership. The final vote was 243 to 172.*

He sensed the smoke before the fire broke out, and thus averted what could have been a travesty.

In the book of Proverbs we read that wisdom, when coupled with prudence, yields knowledge, discretion, and sound judgment.[3] Indeed, if you smell smoke, it's wise to act quickly because there's a good chance fire will follow.

And one more thing. If you take nothing else away from this chapter, remember this:

Don't try to get reimbursed for golf shoes, no matter how green the course may have been.

POINTS TO REMEMBER

★ Even if an answer may seem obvious, don't be afraid to ask a question. Good questions form the foundation of a practical education on the issue at hand.

★ When confronted with a decision, base part of your consideration on what you see, but base your final conclusion also on what you learn after asking the hard questions.

★ Good communication is the art of telling people what they need to know, not what they want to hear.

★ Pay attention to the pulse of your people. Very often, big problems can be prevented if you take the time to handle the small irritants that inevitably emerge in day-to-day business.

PRACTICAL PRINCIPLE #7

MATCH EMOTION FOR EMOTION

*Sincerity makes the very least person to be of
more value than the most talented hypocrite.*
CHARLES SPURGEON

If you will pardon a personal story, I'd like to tell you how a single sentence, penned from the offices of Focus on the Family, once gave me just enough hope at just the right time.

In the summer of 1995, a full two and a half years prior to my move to Colorado Springs, I had submitted an application to Focus on the Family in hopes of landing a job producing the daily radio program. Competition was tough. The interview process was tedious, and the weeks of waiting for an answer soon stretched to months. (This was before Dr. Dobson implemented the policy of communicating with applicants at least once every ten days.) Rather than growing depressed or disappointed with each passing day of silence, however, I actually grew more hopeful. In my mind, the absence of a formal letter of rejection gave me hope. I had done my best, and I was hoping that my best was good enough.

Then one November evening, a thin envelope from Focus on the Family arrived in my mailbox. My heart sank. I knew that thin envelopes usually contained more bad news than good. This letter was no different. My weeks of optimistic theorizing evaporated like the morning fog in San Francisco as I unfolded the single-sheet rejection. So much excited anticipation—now, all down the drain. With a sense of sadness and frustration, I started to toss the letter aside, but a handwritten "P.S." caught my attention and caused me to stop. In blue ballpoint pen was the following concluding thought, written just below the signature:

> Paul—May the Lord continue
> to use you! God bless, *John Fuller*

At the time, I wasn't so sure why those few words did such a good job softening the blow. After all, his message contained none of the standard rejection platitudes designed to make you feel better: "Your resume will be kept for future consideration," or "It was a tough choice." He offered no consolation prize and made no promises. Yet, it seemed to me one of the kindest and most compelling rejection letters I had ever received.

In retrospect, I realize that in his few carefully chosen words, I found empathy, hope, and encouragement. Despite my failure to land a job I so badly wanted, I was comforted by the reminder that a door had closed so another could open someday. John's message was clear: So long as I sought the Lord's direction, the Lord would find a use for me.

In my years of pursuing employment since college, "Thanks, but no thanks" letters were common. Yet, this letter was different from the others. Why? Back in 1995, I didn't know. I do now.

MATCHING EMOTION FOR EMOTION

Since the ministry's inception, Dr. Dobson has insisted on many specific standards of operating procedure, but none stronger than requiring that every piece of correspondence is answered promptly and appropriately with an emotive and sincere tone.

Internally, it's called "matching emotion for emotion"—or *e for e* for short. Dr. Dobson has always believed that for a response to be credible, the wording and motive can't be contrived. At the same time, we can't attempt to use mere platitudes in the hope of winning over the confidence and friendship of the reader. We try to see things from the perspective of the person contacting us— we attempt to understand their hurts or struggles or even their excitement and enthusiasm. By speaking their language, we have a better chance of connecting with the reader, and therefore, we're in a better position to make a difference in his or her life.

What does this mean? If a constituent writes Dr. Dobson a tear-filled, three-page letter lamenting a personal tragedy, he or she will not get a cold form letter in response. Since every situation is different and every challenge is unique, every answer needs to be like a fingerprint: utterly distinct and carefully customized to the person with the need.

Consequently, each piece of correspondence sent to Focus on the Family is read and answered by a real person rather than an automated system. Every letter is acknowledged. If the letter contains a question, the response contains an answer, so long as one is available. If the constituent is asking for a book or tape, we'll do our best to fulfill that request in a timely and efficient manner. But just as important as the response, if not more so, is the sincerity with which it's given. Boilerplate reactions are unacceptable at Focus on the Family. If someone takes the time to write us, we take the time to offer a thoughtful response in return.

Fortunately, Dr. Dobson believes in maintaining this policy of matching emotion for emotion inside Focus on the Family as well, and not only in the form of written communication. Years ago, an employee benevolence fund was created to assist staff members burdened by temporary financial setback. On a purely voluntary basis, employees contribute to the account, and when a need arises, a small committee reviews the situation and will either give an outright gift or offer an interest-free loan to the person seeking assistance.

It's a marvelous program, and one that I can vouch for personally, because I've benefited from it! After only a few months in town, a major car repair put me in a financial hole and I had no idea how I was going to make the monthly rent. Apprehensively, I sought out Sallie Spriggins, the funds facilitator at the time, and told her of my bind. I was embarrassed about having to ask for help, but even more so, I was worried sick over the prospect of being evicted from my apartment. In a loving and gentle manner, Sallie assured me that these types of things happen and told me it was for this purpose that Dr. Dobson first seeded the program with five hundred dollars of his own money.

In retrospect, it's easy to see that Sallie was matching emotion for emotion: She met me where I was at, acknowledged and validated my concern, and offered practical assistance at a time when I needed it most.

CULTIVATING COMPASSION

No matter where they work, most people can identify the things about their job that keep them coming back day in and day out. For some, it's the financial rewards, the convenience of commute, or the match of personal talents with on-the-job responsibilities. Me? I have many, but very high on the list are the people I've worked with over the past seven years. Never have I met a more caring, kind, and friendly group of people. Coincidence? A lucky break? I doubt it.

You see, Focus on the Family is a fine example of just how effective trickle-down sensitivity can be. Soon after being hired, I was told that it would take a few months to be "Focus-ized"—that is, become familiar with the Focus on the Family culture.

At first, I found it unusual to huddle together as a department and pray for a teammate who was struggling with a wayward teenager at home, but I quickly embraced tradition. Over the years, Dr. Dobson has created an atmosphere that encourages and fosters a compassionate spirit among employees. Our departments pray together each morning; we meet as an entire staff for a monthly chapel service; and we receive regular updates about the personal challenges that befall fellow employees. By cultivating compassion internally, it becomes almost second nature to extend the same level of care to constituents in need of assistance.

HISTORY

This is the way things have been done since 1977. As Focus on the Family has grown, so has its attention to the increasing volume of needs delivered to its door on a daily basis. One department—consisting of more than one hundred individuals—now helps Dr. Dobson remain current with his correspondence. This rather complex system may not be the quickest or least expensive way of handling communication, but Dr. Dobson believes it is the right way—and it is consistent with the overall mission of the ministry.

Handling correspondence is a difficult and time-consuming job that could easily be outsourced or done with half the staff if form letters or computer automation were used. But that will never happen so long as James Dobson has breath. In a conversation we had recently, he succinctly summed up his motive behind this policy: "We don't treat people as we do so that they'll like us. We treat people as we do because that's the way the Lord would treat them if He were in our shoes. Our actions don't necessarily reflect Focus on the Family; they reflect God Himself."

THE OTHER END OF THE CONTINUUM

In an ideal world, every piece of correspondence would wind up matching emotion for emotion. That is to say, no matter the circumstance, we'd understand every situation and choose the perfect words in response. Of course, hard as we might try, we often fall short despite our best intentions. Nonetheless, there is a difference between missing the mark by a few feet and missing it by a country mile. According to Dr. Dobson, those who miss it by a mile probably didn't take the time to interpret the multiple layers of the unique communiqué. At Focus on the Family, this type of offense meets with a castigating declaration from Dr. Dobson himself: *Institutional stench!*

In practical terms, this could mean many things. Perhaps the writing sounds rehearsed, as if it's been written a million times. Maybe it sounds canned or syrupy sweet. Sometimes the phrase suggests a lack of warmth and an impersonal tone. Other times it may mean that we've gotten bogged down in corporate or technical lingo.

When identifying institutional stench, Dr. Dobson has been known to use the phrase "dry as dust." This writing contains absolutely no emotion and has failed to connect with the reader. The writer is oblivious to the emotional state of the person or the circumstances surrounding the discussion. The tone is bland and boorish.

Regardless of what kind of writing might elicit the institutional stench moniker, it's safe to suggest that it's writing that needs work! It's ineffective. It has missed the mark and not only will it probably not do any good, it could very well do harm.

All too often, we have only one shot at making a good impression. People draw quick conclusions, and nothing turns someone off more quickly than feigned feelings and obvious insincerity. It is an old saying, but it still rings true: *People don't care how much you know until they know how much you care.*

THE MEASURE OF MODERATION

Even a personal strength, when taken to an extreme often becomes a weakness. Emotion is certainly no different.

It could be said that emotion is the most abused yet under-used component of management and leadership. If harnessed properly, it has the power to move mountains. If neglected, mismanaged, or manipulated, it can devastate a department and crush the human spirit.

In the United States today, most corporations are operating under the illusion that emotion should play a very small role in day-to-day business. This approach ignores the fact that we're all sensitive beings whose production and stability is dependent upon our emotional health.

THE MOOD OF THE MAN

From my vantage point in the executive offices of Focus on the Family, I've seen the many moods of several seasons. These moods have run the gamut from joy to sorrow, from uncertainty to unwavering decisiveness. There have been times of financial plenty and times of fiscal frustration.

One of the more memorable moments came on the morning of September 11, 2001, as I stood with a shaken James Dobson in his office watching the televised coverage of the unfolding carnage in New York City and Washington, D.C.

In stunned disbelief, Dr. Dobson did the only thing he could in an hour of chaos. He called the staff together, and through tears of grief and uncertainty, we prayed. His voice quivered. He was visibly shaken. So were we.

This display of raw, real emotion resonated with the staff. Instinctively, he was matching emotion for emotion. While we all remember the jarring images of the morning, we sometimes forget that in those first few hours and days, additional attacks seemed imminent. Not only were we experiencing grief, but fear as well.

In times of trouble, we look to our leaders, and on the morning of 9/11, Dr. James Dobson ministered to his team of 1,300 people by modeling the best way to deal with devastating circumstances: He prayed.

TOUGH LOVE

Yet another telling moment came when Dr. Dobson discovered that an employee on the staff was having an extramarital affair. He was immediately asked to resign in accordance with Focus on the Family's moral code.

Following the termination, however, Dr. Dobson met separately with the involved parties, hoping to initiate reconciliation for the broken families. A colleague who was present at one of those sessions recalls a James Dobson who was "counselor, pastor, friend, and confidant."

With a tender yet firm countenance, he looked each offending party square in the eye and addressed the matter in a compassionate and convicting manner. He laid out the Scriptures before him and let the Lord's words frame the discussion. From Hebrews, he established the foundational authority of his counsel:

> *If we deliberately keep on sinning after we have received*
> *the knowledge of the truth, no sacrifice for sins is left,*
> *but only a fearful expectation of judgment and of raging*
> *fire that will consume the enemies of God.*
>
> HEBREWS 10:26-27

This was vintage Dr. Dobson. In all conversation, kindness, and in all confrontation, fair-mindedness—but always with the refusal to compromise if a person's actions are in conflict with Scripture.

To James Dobson, matching emotion for emotion doesn't mean placating or patronizing someone; it means identifying the mood of the circumstance and responding in such a way as to make a difference—however unpopular or tough a task it may be.

REAL MEN SHOW EMOTION

One final story is almost too personal to share, but I believe it further illustrates James Dobson's authentic emotivity.

Recently, I was asked to track down some facts that appeared in previous newsletters dating back to the 1980s. I gathered the binders that held each month's copy and settled down at my desk to find the information in question.

As I paged from year to year, my fingers stopped on a letter dated June 26, 1988. The subject: the final days of Myrtle Dobson, Dr. Dobson's mother. It was a heart-wrenching read as he told of how a once active and vibrant woman was now suffering from end-stage Parkinson's disease, lying unresponsive in a coma. (She would pass into heaven just two days later.) Having aging parents in my own family, I could easily place myself in the story. I began to get choked up as the anguish of a man lamenting the loss of his mother became clearer with each passing word.

Midway through the perusal, Dr. Dobson popped his head into my office.

"Have you found it yet?" he asked, referring to the material I had originally been seeking.

"Not yet," I replied, "I was just reading your letter about your mom. It's breaking my heart."

At the mention of his mother, a twinkle came to his eye.

"Make me a copy of that, would you please?" he responded, as he turned on his heels and headed back into his office.

A little over an hour later, he strode back to my desk, the letter rolled up in his hand like a scroll.

"Paul," he said, his voice halting, "she never . . ."

I could see tears welling up in his eyes.

"She never got over the loss of my father. Oh how . . ."

With that, he couldn't offer another word. I stood beside him, my arms folded, shaking my head, empathizing with him but knowing that there weren't any words to offer in consolation.

"I know," I said, "I know."

With a sigh, he smiled. His eyes told the story of a man who missed his mother and who still hurt when he remembered how much his mom had missed her husband during the eleven years between his death and their reunion in heaven.

Here the words of C. S. Lewis ring true: "To love at all is to be vulnerable. Love anything and your heart will certainly be wrung and possibly broken." He went on to conclude that "the only place outside heaven where you can be perfectly safe from all the dangers of love is hell."

In retrospect, I regret not doing what he would have done had the roles been reversed: Hug him! I know that for Dr. James Dobson, when words would fail to match the emotion, nonverbal compassion is equally valued and appropriate.

POINTS TO REMEMBER

The practice of matching emotion for emotion is easier said than done. It occurs more out of habit than happenstance and only when the motive is a desire to help rather than to manipulate someone in the hope that they'll help you. With that in mind, consider these principles when trying to best harness the power of emotion:

★ Effectiveness sometimes comes at the cost of efficiency. It's more important to take your time listening than to answer quickly. Wait to formulate your response until you've fully understood the issue.

★ How you say something is often equally—if not more— important as what you say.

★ Cultivate and invest in your relationships. If you care about a person, you'll find it far easier to practically communicate your care and concern about a problem that comes their way.

★ Emotion is like dynamite. If utilized properly, it can be a force for productive good. If used irresponsibly, it can decimate its recipient.

★ Institutional stench alienates people. Avoid it at all costs.

PRACTICAL PRINCIPLE #8

"HOT, HOT, HOT" ISN'T A THREE-DAY FORECAST IN HAWAII

Success requires both urgency and patience.
Be urgent about making the effort and patient
about seeing the results.
RALPH MARSTON

Of all the businesses in America, the one company that in-trigues and amazes me most is the shipping giant Federal Express.

Its history is a compelling study. In 1965, Yale University undergraduate Frederick W. Smith wrote a term paper high-lighting the need for an airfreight system capable of delivering time-sensitive shipments like medicine, computer parts, and electronics. At the time, putting a man on the moon seemed more plausible than guaranteeing next-day delivery to every city in the country. His professor's skepticism was evident. For his thesis, Smith received a paltry C—though by 1971, he had raised nearly $40 million from investors who saw potential in what most people saw as an impossibility.

Today, this once far-fetched scheme of Frederick Smith yields $23 billion a year in revenue. Logistically speaking, the venture requires enormous daily effort. Consider the facts:

On a typical night, 14,000 employees move 5 million packages via 135 planes, which move through the company's 398-acre national hub in Memphis, Tennessee. Once on the ground, nearly 70,000 trucks finalize the timely distribution of assorted cargo. In the words of a FedEx representative, the nightly scene is of one "controlled chaos" that's managed by both brains and brawn. In the world of Federal Express, the envelope that contains the birthday card to a mother in Missouri is as significant as the vaccine bound for Virginia. Every package is as important as the next.

PRIORITIES

By all accounts, Dr. James Dobson considers every issue that rises to his attention important and worthy of personal review. Yet, the dilemma that faces those with a penchant for detail is often a matter of organization and prioritization. If *everything* is deemed important and urgent, how does one know what to handle first? This is a good question, and it can be easily answered by reviewing Dr. Dobson's internal prioritization system.

First, some background. On a much smaller scale, James Dobson's office sometimes resembles Federal Express's Memphis complex at midnight. The typical day seems to get busier the later the hour gets. The broadcast slated for the next day might require a last-minute edit to reflect an unfolding development. An evening news program might call and invite Dr. Dobson on that night's program for a question-and-answer session. Congressional representatives often contact him to either pitch or plead their case on pending legislation that's relevant to the mission of the ministry. Family members will call; friends will stop by. To put it in more practical terms, *everything* is deadline oriented and *everything* needs to get done.

Throughout the day, Jim Dobson is a man who moves and acts with pinpoint precision. (Internally, we've often joked that he's a "weapon of mass instruction"!) His actions are careful and cautious. When engaged in an assignment, he is intense, focused, and driven. Once he was so engrossed in a writing project that when his wife, Shirley, entered the room and called his name, he nearly jumped out of the chair. Whatever job he is currently doing has his total attention at that moment.

People often remark about Dr. Dobson's enormous capacity for work. It's not that his hours are that much longer than most. He works quickly and efficiently, shifting rapidly from one responsibility to another. I have seen him deeply engrossed at his desk one moment, and five minutes later, waving to some guests from his car in the parking lot as he makes his way home for dinner.

CRACKING THE CODE

Since not everything—no matter how crucial it may be—can possibly be done at the same time, at least not by the same person, Dr. Dobson long ago implemented a three-tiered code of prioritization. Projects are labeled in the following manner, along with their corresponding definition:

- **Hot**—Please hurry!
- **Hot, Hot, Hot**—Please hurry, hurry, hurry!
- **Hottest**—Please hurry, or (in the words of Donald Trump), "You're fired!"

Does this sound harsh? It's really not, and here's why:

Dr. Dobson is not a brute who's bolstered by his own sense of self-importance. He doesn't suffer from the "tyranny of the urgent," nor does he feel like the busier he is, the greater the glory he's bound to receive. He doesn't spin our wheels for the sake of busyness.

Indeed, the motives behind this heart-palpitating pace revolve around respect—respect for the individual, the ministry, and the mission at large. As it is, the present size of the organization, coupled with its established standards, leaves Dr. Dobson very little room for inefficiency! As an organization grows, so does its need for proficiency.

Yet beyond necessity, the reasons for the prioritization structure run deep. He requires promptness from his staff because procrastination reflects poorly on both personal and ministerial performance. While God often requires His people to be patient with Him in matters of faith, He doesn't expect us to *deliberately* delay fulfilling the rudimentary requests of others. Putting it another way, unless the human holdup is unavoidable, the act itself may be disrespectful to the individual left waiting.

COLORFUL EXPRESSIONS

Twenty-year veteran Diane Passno, an executive vice president at Focus on the Family, has devised her own system to manage the expectations of Dr. Dobson's "hot" classifications: "I just decided to treat *everything* as hot," she told me recently in a half-joking manner. "That way, I'll never be caught off guard."

To further delineate the degree of deadline associated with each project, Diane places every assignment into one of three folders. Items in the red folder require immediate attention, those in the yellow stack are nearly as important, and those in the blue portfolio receive careful but more relaxed consideration. Given the voluminous amounts of paper that cross her desk, it's a system that's worked wonders, increasing both productivity and efficiency.

MOUNTING MAIL

Focus on the Family vice president of media relations Paul Hetrick tells a story that goes back to the early days when Focus on the Family was headquartered in California. After being out of the office on several business trips, Paul began to notice opened pieces of mail in his box when he returned to work. At first, he suspected that a mail-sorting machine had grabbed the envelopes and inadvertently broken the seal. Upon closer inspection, however, it became obvious that somebody had been personally opening the envelopes with a finger. And not every envelope either, just a selected assortment.

Irritated at this perceived sense of privacy violation, Paul paid a visit to the post office to inquire about what recourse he might have should the offender ever be caught. "Isn't this illegal?" Paul asked. "No," came the official reply, "once mail is received by a business, anyone is allowed to open it regardless of who it might be addressed to." Despite Paul's frustration, he had no recourse for running the perpetrator up the river.

It didn't take long for the great mail mystery to be solved. Care to take a guess who the culprit turned out to be? Of course—it was James C. Dobson, Ph.D.

Concerned that constituents were being kept waiting for a response, Dr. Dobson often took the liberty of checking the correspondence if he noticed an unopened envelope sitting in the same place for an extended period of time. Neurotic? No. Fastidious? Yes. He's not afraid to push his employees in order to treat the constituent in a manner befitting the mission of the organization.

To James Dobson, the pursuit of healthy behavior has always been a matter of finding the right balance. His first book, *Dare to Discipline*, featured the difficult struggle that parents face in finding the right balance between *love* and *control*. Too much or too little of either principle and the scale is tipped, with failure sure to follow. In this particular situation, Dr. Dobson was doing his best to balance Paul's privilege with that of a constituent's need. He saw beyond the territorial nature of the issue and acted according to conscience. Sure, Paul might have initially been upset, but because of Dr. Dobson's strong sense of priorities, the constituent was well served and so was the cause for Christ.

POINTS TO REMEMBER

★ People will naturally procrastinate unless they're given a plan to prevent it.

★ Avoid procrastination and you'll have time for the projects you really want to do.

★ Assignments that are completed promptly reflect positively on the individual as well as the organization and the cause.

★ Deadlines should not be seen as demons to be feared but rather as the best defense against disaster.

★ In matters of administration, the larger the organization, the more efficient it needs to be in order to be effective.

★ Leaders let their people know what's most important to both them and the organization.

PRACTICAL PRINCIPLE #9

RETURN YOUR CALLS TODAY AND YOU'LL HAVE A JOB TOMORROW

The greatest ability is dependability.
DR. BOB JONES SR.

Around the office, it's known as the principle of the million-dollar mistake.

Here it is in practical and simple terms: Any employee of Focus on the Family can—innocently or unknowingly—make a mistake costing the ministry upwards of one million dollars and keep their job. However, if an employee doesn't return phone calls or fails to answer letters or e-mail from a constituent, that person had better not count on a paycheck for very long.

As far as I can gather, no one has ever tested the veracity of this policy by blowing a cool million dollars of the budget. Nevertheless, I don't doubt for a moment that the code still stands. That's because, if you've been reading this book from the beginning, you're no doubt starting to see a rather predictable pattern developing regarding the issue of respect. Of all the honorable traits that an employee can possess, consideration and respect for others remain of paramount importance to Dr. James Dobson.

It's a required quality because it is the hinge on which good customer service swings.

SETTING THE STANDARD

From the ministry's inception, Dr. Dobson has backed up this commitment to the worth of every individual by establishing and following two foundational principles. Though you'll never see these two signs posted, they can be seen in the actions and reactions of every employee on campus. These principles are applicable no matter the line of work or scope of responsibility. With more than 250,000 people contacting Focus on the Family each month with various requests, we try never to say, "We don't know," "We can't help—go somewhere else." That's why on these two standards there will be no compromise:

> We will always treat people right.
> We will never promise something that we can't deliver.

These simple but forthright statements have served the mission well. However, it hasn't always been smooth sailing. There have been bumps in the road. With more listeners in the 1980s came more mail, and with more mail came the need for more employees. As the staff grew, Dr. Dobson became increasingly concerned that standards were slipping and constituents were being poorly served in the process. He decided one day to nip the issue in the bud by writing a frank, open letter to the staff to share his concern.

Over the course of the past twenty-seven years, James Dobson has written several notable memos—some of which you'll be reading in the later chapters of this book. They are rare and reserved for significant circumstances. Rather than simply summarizing what he wrote, allow me to share parts of this internal staff memo, published for the first time here. Incidentally, this memo was written after a manager resigned, leaving a big stack of old, unopened mail in her desk. This is what precipitated the tone of the memo. It depicts a man unapologetically committed to the goal of treating people right.

FOCUS ON THE FAMILY

M E M O

DATE: April 7, 1986
TO: Supervisors, Managers, Directors, V.P.s, A.D., Correspondence
FROM: Dr. Dobson
RE: Letters sent to departments for response!

An administrative problem has resurfaced here at Focus that should have been solved in 1978.

Unfortunately, it is alive and well to this moment. The difficulty involves letters that the Correspondence department sends to various departments for response but which never return . . . or else they are sent back very late and only after many requests. It should not be Diane's [Passno] responsibility to beg for cooperation in answering these letters, yet that is the position she's in. In some cases, guilty parties have said, "Enough is enough. We'll get it done. Stop bugging us," followed by another burst of inertia. It happens every week. The Publications and Broadcasting departments are the worst offenders, but *every* department is implicated. This time, I am determined to lay the matter to rest.

First, let me express a philosophy about which I feel very strongly. Focus on the Family is a detail organization. The amount of mail we receive and the lives we touch have made us a ministry to more than 900,000 people . . . almost a million families which ask for our assistance and share their burdens with us day after day. Furthermore, the various activities and programs we offer are composed of countless individual parts that must all be accounted for if we are to do the job efficiently. Therefore, I must emphasize that there is *NO* place in this ministry for any employee who is unwilling to chase detail. From vice presidents to the newest hourly employee, we all must be willing to pay that price. I have profound respect for the people who pay our bills and we *will not* treat them shabbily. For every letter which sits at someone's desk, there is a person somewhere who feels insulted or rejected or angry at us for our lack of consideration.

This is a ministry dedicated to Jesus Christ, and nothing short of excellence will prevail . . . especially when we are serving the public.

Detail! Detail! Detail! I know it's frustrating and I'm drowning in it. But if I can chase it, you can too.

Sincerely,
James C. Dobson, Ph.D.
President

Can you sense the passion within his words? Here was a man willing to be temporarily unpopular with his staff—people he loved dearly—for the sake of treating people he barely knew with the respect he felt was due them. He was willing to stir things up in order to settle a persistent problem once and for all.

Like the apostle Paul wrote to the churches of Galatia, "Am I now trying to win the approval of men, or of God?" Paul's response to his own rhetorical query should be ours as well: "If I were still trying to please men, I would not be a servant of Christ" (Galatians 1:10).

MORE TOUGH TALK

By now you're probably convinced that James Dobson isn't a pushover, but I also hope you're not thinking that he's some hot-tempered tyrant who rules with an ironclad fist. Nothing could be further from reality. While he's not prone to stir up trouble, if trouble comes to him, he deals with it swiftly and directly.

Some years back, Dr. Dobson began picking up on a growing sense of arrogance surrounding a particular employee. This staff member had the tendency at times to act like the rooster who took credit for the sunrise. He was unbearable. It all came to a head in the midst of a morning meeting. Mind you, James Dobson is not the type of man to make a habit of "dressing people down" in front of others. Yet in a diplomatic and calm but pointed tone, here is what he said to this boastful individual: "If you think you're irreplaceable," he said, his voice gaining an edge, "you just stick your fist in a bucket of water and see how fast it fills back up when you pull your hand out."

Message delivered, message received.

When it comes to confrontation, Dr. Dobson takes his cue from Scripture. In Proverbs, we're taught that "a patient man calms a quarrel" (Proverbs 15:18), and indeed, I can attest to the fact that James Dobson has a slow rise to anger. In my years working for him, I've never heard him yell or even remotely raise his voice. Here, the fruit of the spirit (Galatians 5:22-23)—love, joy, peace, patience, kindness, goodness, faithfulness, gentleness, and self-control—remain his most potent tools in times of conflict or frustration.

WHEN THINGS GO WRONG

We've established that Dr. Dobson is not afraid to confront attitudes of defiance, laziness, and arrogance, but how does he react when a good and honest effort simply goes bad? This may be one of his most telling qualities of all.

In my first year in the chairman's office, a colleague passed on some sound and valuable advice. How grateful I now am that he did. This is what he said to me: "If you make a mistake, no matter how big or small, admit your error, apologize, and suggest a solution to the problem you created. Then move on. We *all* make mistakes." While advice like that is as old as the hills, it's becoming increasingly countercultural in today's way of thinking. In fact, my friend and colleague Marlen Wells often jokes that while serving on the Toronto police force, many of his partners adhered to a three-tiered response when facing a gaffe or goof-up:

Act surprised. Show concern. Deny everything!

If a Focus staff member ever tried to pull a stunt like that with Dr. Dobson, he'd see through it quicker than he would a clear glass window. He'd smell the smoke, find the fire—and make the necessary adjustments to make sure it didn't happen again. Denial is a dishonest and ill-advised strategy. It never solves the problem, and the people who refuse to own up to their mistakes are soon problems themselves. Dr. Dobson realizes that and thus rewards the straight shooter with seemingly limitless grace.

WILL I EVER LEARN?

When traveling, Dr. Dobson likes to take his laptop computer with him and utilize the time spent in the air or waiting on the ground to work on his current writing project.

Since his monthly newsletter or the average book manuscript may go through dozens of drafts, it's my responsibility as his assistant to make sure the current document he's working on is loaded and accessible prior to departure. It's an easy job, but before the boss used e-mail, it was one that often plagued me because of simple human error and downright forgetfulness.

Let's flash back to a Saturday afternoon two summers ago. While I was laying a stone patio in our backyard, my wife, Julie, brought me the phone and announced that it was Dr. Dobson calling from California.

"Hello, Doctor!" I answered enthusiastically. "How goes it?"

"We've had a great time out here, Paul," he said, "and now we're at the airport waiting for our flight home. But say, I'm trying to find the current draft of next month's newsletter that I asked you to put on the computer last week. Do you recall what folder you put it in? I finally have four free hours to work, and I'm anxious to get started."

My heart sank as I recalled the day he asked me to do it. Chasing the details for a last-minute broadcast had occupied the majority of my time that day, and as he spoke, I realized that I had never loaded the draft.

"Oh brother," I said. "You know what? I forgot to do it! I am sorry. There's no excuse. I blew it."

As quickly as I finished talking, Dr. Dobson responded.

"That's okay, Paul," he said, in a patient and gentle tone. "I know mistakes happen. Please just try and remember to always make sure that when I leave on a trip my computer has the latest versions of what I'm working on."

I wish I could say that was the last blunder related to his computer, but it wasn't. Prior to a trip Dr. Dobson took to Canada, I inadvertently put a document in a folder that wasn't accessible off campus. Again I explained the mistake, and again one would have thought it was the first time I had blown it!

You see, as tough and tenacious as Dr. Dobson may be, he forgives and forgets very easily too. In many ways, he reminds me of the football coach who drives his players hard in practice, trying to get the best out of them in the game, but who is also there to put an arm around the kicker who misses a game-winning field goal as time expires.

DIDN'T ANYONE EVER HEAR OF SPELCHEK?

Each Christmas, Jim Dobson has made a tradition of giving his latest book as a gift to approximately two thousand friends of Focus on the Family. A message is included on a decorative bookplate just inside the front cover and signed personally by Dr. Dobson. It's a time-consuming project on all accounts but one that is very much appreciated by those who receive the present.

In December of 1998, the ink from Dr. Dobson's two thousandth signature had just dried when Focus employee Pam Grettenberger noticed a problem with the message on the bookplate. Despite all of the eyes on the project, nobody—not even Dr. Dobson himself—had noticed that the word *generosity* had been spelled incorrectly within the text of the greeting! All those hours of signing were now for naught.

Executive vice president Tom Mason was chosen to deliver the bad news. Walking into the president's office, Tom didn't offer any excuses, he just told him the facts. What was Dr. Dobson's reaction? "Well, Tom," he said, "I'm glad you caught the mistake before the mailing went out." Graciously, he didn't point any fingers, but instead accepted the news and didn't gripe or growl.

A similar incident occurred in March of 2003 when the monthly newsletter had just come off the presses. As a tribute to Shirley Dobson's stepfather, Joe Kubishta, color photographs were placed throughout the letter. When I delivered a copy of the letter to Dr. Dobson, he questioned the tint of the paper. "It's yellow as though it were old!" he said disgustedly. "Really?" I countered. "I thought it looked okay." Sure enough, when I compared it to a previous month, the paper was more yellow than white. After looking into how it happened, I discovered that because I hadn't told our print buyer in time that we'd be printing in color, the vendor hadn't had enough time to order a higher quality paper. Sheepishly, I went back to Dr. Dobson, told him what had happened, apologized, and informed him that from this point forward, we'd be getting paper samples before each color print job. He was satisfied. "Okay," he said, "that's good. Mistakes happen."

Indeed, mistakes do happen in every line of work. It's never a question of *if* a mistake will happen; it's a matter of how you will react and what you will do when the error occurs.

POINTS TO REMEMBER

★ Focus on humility. Worry less about yourself and more about others.

★ Chase the detail, and problems are less likely to chase after you.

★ Focus on dependability. Dependability is more admirable than intelligence or ability.

★ If you make a mistake, admit it, apologize, and work toward a solution—not a clever excuse.

★ And one final thing: Return your phone calls!

PRACTICAL PRINCIPLE #10

LEAVE TERRITORIALISM
OFF THE TABLE

Self-interest is the enemy of all true affection.
PRESIDENT FRANKLIN D. ROOSEVELT

We open with an observation: The more times change, the more things remain the same. Let's see if you can find the common thread woven throughout this eclectic assortment of stories:

- More than 3,300 years ago, a young Pharaoh by the name of Akhenaton instigates an Egyptian religious revolution by declaring the supremacy of a single god: Aten, the god of the sun. The polytheistic majority begins calling for his head.
- In 1984, Andrew "Fat Boy" Doyle and five members of his family are murdered in Glasgow, Scotland, because they refuse to stop delivering ice cream to certain parts of the city. An industry competitor is found guilty of killing the six by burning down their house.
- In Santa Cruz, California, surfers and surf kayakers just can't seem to get along, threatening each other with lawsuits over the rights to—believe it or not—the waves of the ocean.

- Following the terrorist attacks of 9/11, U.S. officials try to explain why the CIA hadn't been sharing intelligence information with the FBI and why the FBI hadn't been sharing its findings with the CIA.

THE LINK

Each of these situations, ranging from the serious to the silly, are all examples of what is commonly called a turf war, or territorial dispute. As you can see, this is an age-old problem and the source of great angst in the workplace, the church, the neighborhood, and even a seemingly peaceful beach! In every one of the four anecdotes mentioned above, someone either had what the other person wanted or wanted rights to what the other person did. It always follows the same pattern.

Why? One of the main problems is that human nature instinctively feeds this weakness. Just look around. We lay claim to our possessions by building fences around our houses and putting locks on our doors. We're marking territory. We're fiercely protective and naturally individualistic at the core of our being. We defend our little corner of the world even though as Christians we know deep down that everything is on loan and nothing is personally owned. Nonetheless, we get reeled in quickly.

Sometimes even widely accepted values seem to be in contradiction with each other. As we discussed in the last chapter, it's a good thing to take ownership of an issue and accept responsibility for getting a job done. Yet if we take it too far, if we hold things too tightly, we run the risk of becoming territorial, egotistical, and not very fun to work with. What gives? Again, it comes down to finding the right balance. How much control is too much? How little interest is not enough? As the entrepreneurial founder of Focus on the Family, Dr. Dobson is familiar with the complex challenges associated with territorial-minded people.

THE CYCLE OF AN ORGANIZATION

It's been said that some entrepreneurial founders tend to be like root-bound plants. They birth an organization and maintain such a viselike grip on the management and development of the institution that there's little room for growth. Out of a fear of competition or a desire to retain absolute control, they don't hire many new people. Subsequently, there's a void of creativity, perspective, and objectivity. When this happens, the influence of the organization inevitably declines, and often the group ceases to exist within a few years.

Of course, this type of demise and decline isn't always the case, and it's certainly not so in the case of James Dobson and Focus on the Family. Naturally, the question begs to be asked, *So, what makes this entrepreneurial founder so different from the rest?* It's a good question with an interesting answer.

THE PROFILE

Dr. James Dobson is a modest but confident man. He takes risks. He runs fast. He's creative, strong willed, persistent—and not easily intimidated. Given some of these attributes, it shouldn't surprise you to learn that in the early days, James Dobson tended to hire people who were a lot like himself. In return, the various departments were headed by competent, ambitious, passionate, and hard-driving people. They tended to be racehorses rather than oxen. This was a good thing, but like anything else, it wasn't perfect.

Unfortunately, a few of these same hardworking people took some of these same generally admirable characteristics to an unhealthy extreme. We're all vulnerable to such behavior, but entrepreneurial people seem to run the greatest risk due to an instinctual and passionate spirit. To cite the previous analogy, some people are better on the track then they are back at the barn. Generally speaking, territorial-minded people don't regularly delegate responsibility. They manipulate, hoard, or withhold information and enjoy being seen as the lone source for every answer involving their specialty. Controlling people forge strategic alliances with some and shun those they see as a threat to their position. Intimidation is a popular tactic in the toolbox of territorial people. They tend to be self-centered souls who want to take all of the credit when things go well but none of the blame when the situation goes bad. They are a cancer in the organization.

While these types of people by no means dominated the organization, a few of them did exist, and they caused trouble disproportionate to their overall numbers. Dr. Dobson used to call these pockets of resistance *silos* because the people within them were operating separately from the rest of the organization. They may just as well have been doing nothing at all because by their self-imposed alienation, they were doing more harm than good.

Fortunately, these were rare occurrences, but rare as they were, they had great potential to impair the effectiveness of Focus on the Family. To protect against the proliferation of varying factions, Dr. Dobson has always had an open-door policy. He'll "talk to anyone, at any time—about anything!" There is no hiding place if the boss holds to a promise like that.

James Dobson has always let it be known that he doesn't want his employees to think they have a personal piece of the pie. "The Lord owns it all," he has said hundreds of times. "If the Lord told us to close our doors, we would do just that." Of course, steering clear of a territorial mentality often requires deliberate and conscious action.

GOOD CREDIT

During his presidency, Ronald Reagan kept a powerful reminder of this principle on his desk in the Oval Office. On a plaque, visible to all who entered, were these words: "There is no limit to what a man can do or where he can go if he doesn't mind who gets the credit." Indeed, this is a lesson and motto played out every day in the office of James Dobson in various ways.

As I mentioned earlier, Focus on the Family receives approximately a quarter million inquiries each month, and every single one of them receives a specialized response according to the nature of the request. Naturally, Dr. Dobson can't answer all of those letters personally, but correspondence assistants respond on his behalf after first consulting with his published writings and teachings on the subject in question.

At first glance, that might seem efficient—and it is—but I've been struck by the fact that all of these letters go out under the signature of the assistant, not Dr. Dobson. Have you ever written to your senator or congressman? The reply you receive is always signed by the representative, but you know he never wrote the letter and probably never saw it! Politicians want the visibility and the credit. But not James Dobson. Getting the information and advice to the constituent in a timely fashion is the important thing; who gets the credit for writing the letter is not.

Here's another example. Recently, Dr. Dobson finished writing the book *Marriage Under Fire*. A timely project given the politically charged atmosphere surrounding the institution of marriage, he completed the manuscript in a matter of weeks, pouring every ounce of available energy into the undertaking. So quick was the process that the publisher hadn't even suggested contractual terms regarding the book until the manuscript was nearly done. When the publisher did call to discuss the terms, Dr. Dobson invited me into his office to be part of the negotiations.

It was a wonderfully encouraging experience, and in retrospect, I wish I had asked permission to tape it. As Don Jacobson, the publisher at Multnomah Publishers, laid out the details surrounding the project—the deadlines, the number of copies in the first print run, the promotional efforts—Dr. Dobson listened intently, taking notes and asking a couple of clarifying questions. When the topic turned to compensation, Dr. Dobson simply waved his hand in the air and said, "Don, I've decided to donate every cent of the royalties from this book to Focus on the Family. This issue is the big one, and we're going to need every available resource to fight. I can't take anything for this effort. The battle belongs to the Lord." As the conversation concluded, Don expressed his appreciation for Dr. Dobson's tireless efforts on the book, given how many adjustments he had made to his schedule in order to make this venture a reality. As he's prone to do, Dr. Dobson graciously passed the credit on to his assistant sitting on the other side of the desk!

To me, this sacrificial and humble spirit of a leader speaks volumes about the overall character of the man and his ability and desire to simply get the job done.

First, the financial issue. While Dr. Dobson has always donated the royalties from books sold through the ministry to Focus on the Family, he pays his bills and puts food on the table with the resources from his works sold elsewhere. Since he doesn't draw a salary, this is his sole source of income. Second, and more importantly, this conversation illustrated again Dr. Dobson's belief that it's more important to accomplish a goal—in this case, the preservation of marriage—than it is to receive personal gain for leading the charge.

Indeed, the words memorialized on the plaque on President Reagan's desk bear repeating: "There is no limit to what a man can do or where he can go if he doesn't mind who gets the credit."

MANY HANDS—ONE MISSION

Dr. Dobson is famous for reminding his radio listeners that he's "not a one-man band." Believe it or not, there are those who listen infrequently to his radio broadcast who think Focus on the Family consists of merely Dr. Dobson, cohost John Fuller, and maybe a part-time secretary to answer the phone. Hardly! The organization may run lean for reasons of good stewardship, but many hands touch what you might otherwise consider to be a simple project. Good things happen because good people work together as a team.

To illustrate this point, take a look at the following snapshot of those who help Dr. Dobson with his monthly letter. This is by no means an exhaustive listing, but it does affirm the fact that turf wars won't be won in the office of James Dobson.

Deb Butterfield is responsible for making sure all supplies for the letter are ordered and received and that the project stays on the schedule that **Jack Hoffman** plans out each month. **Paul Vorreiter** and **Beau Henderson** lay out the letter and design the envelope and artwork for each month's mailing. **Sherry Cisneros** negotiates the quantity and price for the paper. **Jon Vaughan, Glenn Peterson,** and **Herb Burnham** are responsible for pulling together the numerous mailing details, such as the 2.5 million addresses and envelope inserts. **Kathy Peterson** and her team in the warehouse collate the letters and get them ready for shipment. **John Klotz** and **Pam Grettenberger** coordinate legal business with the United States Postal System. **Barb Isaacson** and **Terri Art** determine what book offers should accompany the mailing. **Chad Hills** and **Glenn Stanton** in our public policy division double-check all the footnotes and facts within the letter itself.

I'm sure you get the picture. Just imagine what could happen if any one of these fine individuals decided to become territorial so far as their responsibilities go. Every one of these folks completes a task necessary to the mailing. They are a small spoke in a big wheel. If Sherry began getting into contractual disputes with the paper vendor, there wouldn't be any paper to print on. If Chad or Glenn decided they didn't like the way Dr. Dobson worded a sentence and changed it without going through proper channels, the newsletter could be subject to a higher postage rate for legal reasons, costing the ministry an extra million dollars. More importantly, if any of these people become territorial, the entire process is held up, and the entire month's mailing would be put in jeopardy! But because these faithful servants do their job, I'm able to do mine.

Teamwork trumps territorialism every time.

POINTS TO REMEMBER

★ Take your responsibilities seriously, but don't be too serious about your own sense of self-importance.

★ Hold everything with an open hand. Territorialism develops by hanging on to things too tightly.

★ Good teams develop when teammates aren't concerned about who gets credit for success.

★ Most organizations don't fall as a result of outside competitors but instead from internal turf wars.

IN ALL THINGS, REACH FOR EXCELLENCE

I have the simplest tastes. I am always
satisfied with the best.
OSCAR WILDE

To Dr. James Dobson, mediocrity is the measure of a job half done. What many deem satisfactory, he considers second-rate. What some judge as good, he often regards as not good *enough*. That's because he sees success not simply by the outcome but by the standards and quality of the pursuit. If something is worth doing at all, it's worth doing well. That's why in his office, every job, no matter how simple or complex, large or small, must be done with an uncompromising commitment to excellence.

SLIPPING STANDARDS

Excellence isn't so easy to come by these days. In 2003, the Gallup Organization released the results of a workplace survey. According to the findings, 71 percent of U.S. workers admitted that they were "not engaged" in their current jobs. Despite the lackluster effort, they were, of course, still committed to collecting and cashing their paychecks. Perhaps even more disturbing, however, was another finding of the study. Many of the disgruntled employees who were working at call centers admitted that they *deliberately* irritated and provoked customers in an attempt to get them off the phone more quickly! Remember that the next time you call a company with a service complaint.[4]

Slacking off at the office has now become popular sport. Two of the most common Web sites regularly accessed by the disengaged worker are aptly named www.ishouldbeworking.com and www.boredatwork.com. It would be funnier if it weren't so sad. Replete with games, jokes, surveys, and message boards, the sites even contain "panic buttons" that will immediately redirect your computer to a business-oriented site in the event that your boss walks in while you're surfing the day away.

One survey found that 59 percent of sales online were conducted from work.[5] Granted, a good amount could be work-related, but considering the fact that www.ebay.com and www.americansingles.com rated highest in traffic, one is left with the assumption that much of the Internet activity is purely personal.

Lest you think the slacker phenomenon is limited to the United States, it should be noted that a contingent in Great Britain celebrates National Slacker Day each August. The motto speaks for itself: "Stand up for your right to sit back down again." Though he's an admirer of the English culture for its long and storied history, I assure you this is one holiday that Dr. Dobson won't be celebrating!

IS HARD WORK HARMFUL?

Okay, so we've established that a strong work ethic has taken a beating in *some* sectors of society. On the other end of the spectrum, of course, you can easily find an army of raging workaholics who live at the office and do little more than toil away at their desk. In some ways, both types of workers suffer from a similar malady: lack of balance. The quality of work is compromised on either end of the continuum. Sluggards don't get things done, but stressed and harried people don't get things done well. The pursuit of excellence is a habit best wrought by balancing persistence, insistence, and consistency.

Dr. Dobson tells of a conversation he had with a physician friend some years ago. At the time, he was busier than a barber at boot camp and keeping extremely long hours. His energy and productivity were high, but he wondered if his pace could be a problem.

"Is hard work harmful?" he asked his friend.

The doctor assured him that it wasn't. "Oh no!" replied the physician, "Hard work will actually *keep you alive!* The problem comes when you can't find the time to recover in between the busy stretches. Work hard, but rest regularly."

That's good advice, because it actually comes from God Himself. If even the Creator of the universe rested on the seventh day, how much more must *we* need recuperation to find a sense of refreshment?

Jim Dobson loves a Sunday afternoon nap. He's also a voracious recreational reader who finds much relaxation in a good book and an easy chair. One of my favorite questions for him is, "What are you reading these days?" Often, he'll let me borrow the book when he's done—I always enjoy seeing his underlines and notes in the margin as I read along.

PAYING THE PRICE

Dr. Dobson sees the road to excellence as a path paved by a series of small steps consisting of attention to detail and a willingness to pay the price in terms of time, effort, and commitment. This is a talk that he walks.

Paul Hetrick tells of watching Dr. Dobson "wind down" on the way home from an exhausting weeklong trip to Washington, D.C. While the rest of the staff was kicking back on the plane ride home, maybe reading a *Sports Illustrated,* doing a crossword puzzle, or taking a nap, James Dobson's routine was very different. Here are Paul's words:

> *Just as soon as the plane leveled off, Dr. Dobson lowered his tray table and began digging into his suit-coat pockets, pulling out piles of receipts that he had accumulated from the previous week's worth of travel. Lodging, food, transportation—they were all in one big stack. He would then spread them out and begin sorting. Some were personal expenses, but the majority were business related. This was in the day before computers spelled out the exact source of the expense, so there was more room for error than there is now. When I asked him why he didn't just wait until he got home, he told me, "If you're not filling out your expense report within the first forty-eight hours after your trip, you're just making it up!"*

Dr. Dobson doesn't make up anything, and because of his visible example to his staff, they began working on *their* expense report long before the details may have been otherwise lost to memory.

PATIENCE AND PERSISTENCE

As a writer and broadcaster, James Dobson's life revolves around deadlines. Thirty minutes of air must be filled each day with quality programming. Publishers demand the finished product sometimes faster than he can write it.

This may be understandable, but the problems associated with deadlines shouldn't be understated. If not managed properly, deadlines can sometimes tempt a person to settle for a subpar effort in exchange for moving the burden off their back. It's an understandable urge, but it's a response I've never seen James Dobson employ. Quality within the context of deadlines is possible as long as you're willing to work hard and pay the price in personal effort.

Every month, Dr. Dobson writes a letter to approximately 2.5 million people. It's a project that consumes a great deal of his time and requires a significant amount of his effort. It's rarely finalized until the eleventh hour. Internally, we keep score on the number of drafts each letter goes through. During my tenure, I've seen him revise a letter twenty-seven times one month and twenty-four times another. If he's not happy with the product and the deadline is upon us, we'll move the deadline so as not to compromise the quality of the letter.

The same rings true for his book writing. By now, an author of his caliber could hire a ghostwriter and publish a book every three months. Or he could get away with turning out an inferior product and allowing his name to sell it instead of the substance of the subject. I assure you this will never happen! Every word in every book Dr. James Dobson writes flows directly from his heart through to his pen. It's the way he is wired and he won't work any other way. If circumstances begin to compromise the quality, he'll stop writing until a time when he can give his full attention to the project.

For example, he recently rewrote one of his earliest best sellers, *The Strong-Willed Child*. He had planned to finish the project over the course of a summer, but reality proved otherwise. He put it down in July and didn't pick it up again until the fall, simply because he wasn't able to allocate 100 percent of his energy to doing it. Better undone than halfhearted. That's because just doing something good is just not good enough.

DELIGHTING IN THE DETAIL

Dr. and Mrs. Dobson enjoy staying in touch with their many personal friends and supporters of Focus on the Family through the exchange of cards each Christmas. While the concept of choosing, writing, and mailing a card may seem painfully simple, the task of managing over one million Christmas greetings is anything but easy.

Jim Dobson doesn't just hand off responsibilities to a staff member and forget about them. Because he cares about the people who receive the cards, he cares about the process behind the mailing too. His penchant for detail and pursuit of excellence are illustrated perfectly by the many facets—and sometimes the frustrations—associated with the management of the mailing.

Jon Vaughan, the director of constituent marketing at Focus on the Family, has overseen the Christmas card assignment for nearly ten years. Beginning in June, Jon starts the ball rolling by running concepts by Dr. and Mrs. Dobson. "They want to see everything from start to finish," Jon says, "including the designs, the photographs, and even the wording of the cards from previous years. They have meticulous and exacting taste, and we may go back and forth a dozen times before they settle on the card for the season."

For Jon, the effort and even the angst are well worthwhile when he hears later that for some people the card held special meaning. For example, this past year, a postal worker wrote to say that though he had delivered thousands of cards to people on his route, the Dobsons' card was the only one that he had received. Simple joys come when simple tasks are done well.

Sound sappy? Maybe. But just remember: Great things are more likely to happen when good people do their job well.

MEET SECURITY

Do you remember the classic television sitcom *M*A*S*H*? At times, life seems to imitate its satire. In one episode, the irrepressibly neurotic Major Frank Burns, played by actor Larry Linville, complains to Alan Alda's character, Captain "Hawkeye" Pierce, that "I'm only paranoid because everyone is out to get me."

It's a funny line, but unfortunately, we're living in an increasingly dangerous society. Dr. Dobson has received death threats, obscene letters, and all sorts of sordid material designed to intimidate, distract, or simply harass. It can get ugly, but these threats don't work, partly because Dr. Dobson trusts in the Lord's hand of protection and partly because of the confidence he has in his security force. That force consists of four men—Bruce Hoover, Mike Benzie, Den Patterson, and Sam Moore—who protect not only the chairman and his family, but also the entire 1,300-member ministry.

I mention these guys because they epitomize the principle we're discussing. You see, they're not simply bodyguards. Nor are they busybodies, for that matter, who hassle suspicious-looking people. Not at all. In fact, because of their willingness to go the extra mile, active protection has become a minor element of their jobs. They personify the pursuit of excellence because they're always living and thinking one step ahead of everyone else. If they anticipate trouble before trouble goes down, the trouble never sees the light of day.

Let's say Dr. Dobson has a trip planned to Washington, D.C. Prior to his departure, a member of the security team painstakingly prepares for every possible scenario that could be encountered on the trip. The itinerary is broken down like a military operation—not surprising since the chief of security, Bruce Hoover, is a retired Delta Force commando! Driving directions, hotel and restaurant locations, and emergency contingency plans are all part of the advance work for the trip. The security force worries about the details surrounding the travel so that Dr. Dobson can worry about the details related to the trip.

PROFESSIONALISM PAYS OFF

Dr. Dobson's travel schedule increased dramatically in 1996 when he accepted an appointment to the federal gambling commission. His work took him from coast to coast and to every gambling hot spot in between. When he first began attending the meetings, several members of the commission scoffed at the security detail that accompanied him on each trip. Some thought it arrogant; others, wasteful; and some, just plain silly.

But an interesting thing happened. The same people who mocked the presence of the security team began making good use of the men by his side. The members realized that if they stuck with the Focus contingent, they never got lost, they always made it to meetings on time, and they never had to worry about finding a suitable restaurant for meals. The Focus security staff soon became the unofficial security team for the entire commission.

POINTS TO REMEMBER

★ The price of excellence is paid throughout the process; the price of mediocrity is paid long after the process is complete.

★ Hard work isn't harmful so long as you as take the time to rest regularly between projects.

★ Don't let deadlines dictate the quality of your work; let quality dictate the deadlines you agree to adhere to.

★ There is no such thing as a worthless or insignificant detail. The pursuit of excellence is all about chasing down the details that other people might otherwise overlook.

AS GOES YOUR DISCIPLINE, SO GOES YOUR WAY OF LIFE

The first and best victory is to conquer self.

PLATO

If you were to garner a glance at Dr. James Dobson's workout log, you'd find a single, handwritten, two-word phrase peppered repeatedly throughout the calendar. Coming on the heels of long days and short nights, cold mornings and hot summer afternoons, the comment is intensely personal. It reflects neither an ideological stubbornness nor intellectual shortsightedness, but instead a practical quality more valuable than all the cash this country has on hand. Scrawled sporadically but emphatically is this two-word declaration:

No compromise!

What that means is this: *Regardless of circumstance and personal condition and in spite of every possible reason why I could justify skipping a workout today, I won't.* The reasons may be many, but the choices are actually few. It's been said that there are two types of pain in life: the pain of discipline and the pain of regret. Choose your pain; the choice is yours! To those who select wisely, comfort will not come at the cost of conscience. End of story.

To James Dobson, discipline in life is like oil in an engine. It keeps the motor running even when the heat begins to rise. It keeps the train on the tracks. It is the difference between chaos and control.

ORIGINS

The terms *discipline* and *Dobson* have been inextricably linked since 1970. At the time, a young James Dobson saw society beginning to discard and ignore the tried-and-true methods of traditional parenting. In the wake of the 1960s cultural revolution, strict fathers were beginning to be portrayed as fools and mothers as accessories to the crime. Permissive parenting was gaining popularity and even many "experts" in the field of family psychology began weighing the merits of lenient leadership in the home.

This was the world into which Dr. Dobson waded, publishing his first book, *Dare to Discipline.* Having since sold nearly 4 million copies, it obviously struck a powerful chord.

Given the title, the premise is self-explanatory, but the deeper message is often missed by critics who don't see beyond the controversies surrounding corporal punishment. Disciplining children is much more than a debate about spanking. In fact, Dr. Dobson himself will tell you that spanking has more to do with a breakdown in child discipline than it does in the discipline process itself. The effective parent will build a relationship with their child while simultaneously laying down the rules of the home. Without this relationship, rebellion is practically guaranteed. Parents correct because they care, and they care because they want to pass on the virtues of a disciplined demeanor. Likewise, our own personal pursuit of self-discipline throughout our later years finds its roots in behaviors that were instilled in us at a very young age.

Indeed, James Dobson's definition of discipline is rooted in its derivative: the word *disciple,* meaning "to lead to a higher cause," or as another linguist suggests, "a person who believes in and helps disseminate the teachings of a master."[6] Its connotation is far more positive than punitive because, as it says in the book of Isaiah, "Discipline is good, for it leads to life and health" (38:16, NLT). These words carry a very clear scriptural mandate that's applicable to us personally and to those entrusted in our care. If discipline is "the way to life" (Proverbs 6:23, NLT), then it makes good sense to order our days and actions accordingly. If we can't first discipline ourselves in both our thoughts and actions, how can we credibly discipline others? We cannot. Radio commentator Paul Harvey has often prefaced tales of national and personal turmoil by observing that "self-government won't work without self-discipline."

In the life of Dr. James Dobson, be it spiritually, athletically, academically, or personally, self-discipline seems almost second nature. He has always believed in getting his house in order before advising others to do the same.

THE STREAK

To illustrate, let's take another look at the workout log.

As a collegian, a young Jim Dobson lettered all four years in tennis and captained the team as a senior. His regular tennis playing continued through his late thirties until he began enjoying regular games of pickup basketball with friends. "I love the camaraderie of basketball because it's unlike tennis, where it's just you alone," he once told me. This comment speaks well to the man's appreciation for teamwork and the benefits of a cooperative spirit within a working relationship.

Perhaps a younger James Dobson would have felt more inclined to tackle challenges independent of others. After all, when he launched Focus on the Family in 1977, he did so with just himself and a part-time secretary. It was basically a one-man band. No longer. Maturity has proven collaboration to be a key commodity in his arsenal of management tools.

Unfortunately, the game of basketball almost took his life. It was in the middle of a layup that a heart attack struck. Though he fully recovered, his doctors advised him to stay off the court. He did—but he didn't stay off his feet. As he recovered, he began formulating a seventy-minute aerobic and strength-training regimen. Most doctors are lucky to get their patients to work out three days a week. Jim Dobson decided to exercise every day.

The streak began on December 13, 1993. With the exception of a seven-day period in 1998, during which time he suffered and miraculously recovered fully from a major stroke that temporarily left him unable to speak—and one stray day when he was writing and simply forgot to exercise—he has not missed a day. To date, that's nearly four thousand consecutive daily workouts. On one occasion during a trip to the East Coast, he and one of his security men walked the streets of Washington, D.C., at 4 AM (2 AM their time, having just arrived the night before from Colorado) in order to get his exercise done before rushing to an early morning meeting.

Obsessive? No. There is a difference between obsessive behavior and disciplined behavior. Obsessions are characterized by a complete preoccupation with a particular activity that both mentally and physically drains the body of energy. In Dr. Dobson's case, his exercise actually gives him the energy he needs to fulfill a hectic and harried schedule. "Regardless of how I feel when I begin the workout," he says, "I always feel better, more energized, and in a better mood when I'm done." It is the great paradox of energy and exercise. If you think you're too tired to work out, you inevitably discover instead that you're too tired to *not* work out. The investment of time is well worth the rate of return. The pain of discipline yields positive results.

TIME MANAGEMENT

Discipline is not only modeled in action, but also in abstinence. It is turning down certain invitations that you really want to accept. It is realizing that in many cases, too much of something can compromise most of everything. At times, you have to say no so that later on you'll be available to say yes.

With days that begin in the predawn dark and often end under moonlit skies, Dr. Dobson is, simply put, a busy man. Of course, this is not uncommon, but with a worldwide radio audience and a host of other ministerial responsibilities, he has many people vying for his time and attention. His schedule is often booked months in advance. By necessity, he turns down far more engagements than he could ever accept, and because of his nature, he accepts far more than his schedule really should allow. Based on the sheer volume of requests, it would be easy for him to lose control of his calendar if not for the discipline to sometimes say no.

Regardless of personal fortitude and the sincerest of intentions, this is sometimes easier said than done.

Shortly after Christmas 2003, Dr. Dobson was settling back into his Colorado Springs routine after having spent the holidays with his family in California. While most people might return from a vacation refreshed, it was clear to me that his three weeks out west had been anything but restful. Running up against a book deadline, plowing through broadcast preparations, and engaging in intense discussions with Washington lawmakers about the Federal Marriage Amendment— all while on a supposed vacation—had taken an obvious toll.

"You need a vacation to recover from your vacation," I commented at the conclusion of a meeting his first week back. Sitting back in his chair, his desk piled high with unread letters and memos, he smiled. "I wish," he replied, "but there is just so much going on. Shirley and I are going absolutely crazy! We need to get a hold on this before it runs us into the ground."

It was apparent that even for a man with seemingly endless energy, the burdens of the schedule were beginning to hobble his pace.

"Don't you sometimes wish you could simply sit back in the evening with a good book or watch a movie with Mrs. Dobson?" I asked.

Nodding, he put down his pen, folded his hands, and looked off through his window to the northwest. "Shirley and I wish we could just get in the car on a Saturday and drive up to Denver, shop, have lunch, and maybe catch a show at the theater. We haven't even had time to do that. We have got to make some changes."

Disciplined leaders are more likely to sense the train leaving the tracks before it actually does because they're more familiar with the feel of the ride and can sense when even small things are amiss. For James Dobson, one of his first benchmarks is time with his wife. What time is it when an elephant sits on your car? Time to get a new car. Likewise, when Dr. Dobson's work schedule begins to consistently encroach on the weekend, and thus, time with Shirley, it's time to make changes. Quickly.

ADJUSTMENTS

Shortly after our conversation, Dr. Dobson convened a panel of colleagues to help him map out a plan for lightening his schedule a bit. The committee consisted of people who knew him best: Shirley Dobson, the executive leadership, a few longtime friends, and his personal support staff, of which I am a part.

He began the conversation not by lamenting but by reminding the staff of Psalm 139. In part, it reads:

Lord, you have searched me and you know me.
You know when I sit and when I rise; you perceive my
thoughts from afar. You discern my going out and
my lying down; you are familiar with all my ways. . . .

All the days ordained for me were written in your
book before one of them came to be.
PSALM 139:1-3, 16

If there is an omnipotent God watching over the affairs of humankind, it is only right to act according to His will. While the meeting was designed to help reprioritize James Dobson's schedule, this Scripture reminded us that we were really meeting to better understand the priorities of God.

While we may flutter from one task to the next, agonizing over our allotment of time for each project, it is good to remember that we need to first seek counsel from the Source who knows us best. If we can discipline ourselves to pause and pray before we pounce, we will be well served.

As if to remind us of human folly, a staff member interrupted the meeting after just ten minutes to alert Dr. Dobson that a "critical call" was awaiting his attention. He left his own meeting to take the call, even though just moments earlier someone had encouraged him to carve out a daily amount of uninterrupted time. We sat around the table, each seeing the irony of his empty chair in the midst of a meeting about his busy schedule. The silence was soon broken when Del Tackett, an executive vice president at Focus on the Family, quipped, "Well, if the rest of you would leave, I could get through the rest of this agenda and solve all of his problems!"

LESSONS LEARNED

While we didn't completely solve all of the problems associated with the busyness of Dr. Dobson's schedule that day, he did come away from the table with twenty-five suggestions that he deemed helpful and practical. However, the specifics were not as important as the valuable lessons that were gleaned both from this exercise and James Dobson's personal definition of discipline.

POINTS TO REMEMBER

By observing the life of James Dobson, you can see that
self-discipline is not some unattainable or lofty goal but
instead is a deliberate, methodical process comprised
of five main elements:

★ **Attainable Commitments:** Once the goal is identified,
the commitment must be made. Commitments may not
always be popular, but they define a disciplined life.

★ **Reasonable Requirements:** All things in moderation.
While water may be needed for survival, if you get too
much of it you'll invariably drown. If your goals are within
reason, a healthy dose of discipline will keep you in check.

★ **Flexible Adjustments:** The strongest trees are not
always those that stand straight but those that can bend
with the force of the wind. So it is with discipline. When
a wise leader sees his schedule getting out of control,
he doesn't necessarily hunker down for the battle.
Instead, he's humble enough to make necessary adjustments. He is flexible. Discipline is not always doing the
same thing the same way; sometimes it's finding a
different way to ultimately arrive at the same end result.

★ **Manageable Disappointments:** Setbacks are part
of every success. Winners are sometimes one-, two-,
or five-time losers who just never gave up. Discipline
is the momentum that keeps you moving even when
disappointment tries to stop you in your tracks.

★ **Inevitable Contentment:** Self-discipline is the habit
everyone loves to hate. While bad habits may start out
fun, discipline can be a real drag from the very beginning
to very near the end. Discipline is a silent virtue that
often goes unacknowledged for long periods of time.
It is not glamorous. It is not flashy. In the end, however,
there can be no doubt about its lasting value. Simply
put, it feels good to do well.

PRACTICAL PRINCIPLE #13

FORGET THE FLAIR—JUST CARE

The fullest and best ears of corn hang
lowest toward the ground.
EDWARD REYNOLDS

Sometimes, simple stories do a wonderful job revealing and capturing the values of the most complex men.

Take for example, the story of Ronald Reagan's first job. Between 1926 and 1932, the young "Dutch" Reagan worked as a lifeguard on the Rock River in Dixon, Illinois, and saved seventy-seven lives during the seven summers of his service. His pay? Just fifteen dollars a week, plus all the hamburgers, onions, pickles, and root beer that he wanted from the food stand by the shore. With a spirit of self-sacrifice, a young Reagan was known to lay his life on the line in order to ensure the safety of those entrusted to his care. It was a theme consistent over the course of his life. He never viewed public service as a stepping-stone to prosperity, but instead as a privilege of the highest order. From saving swimmers to helping stave off the threat of nuclear annihilation, the essence of Ronald Reagan has always been magnificently simple: safety through strength, strength through service.

From the day I first met him, I saw these types of "Reaganesque" characteristics in Dr. James Dobson. While he may never have been a lifeguard in the same way as our former president, he has been a vigilant guarder of life for those unable to defend themselves. Revealed, of course, in different settings and circumstances, he and former President Reagan shared a demeanor and discipline of similar order.

FIGHTING FOR THE UNDERDOG

Shortly before Christmas a few years ago, I found myself waiting for Dr. Dobson in his office. While I was waiting, I passed the time by looking at some of the framed pictures on the shelf behind his desk. My eyes stopped on the photograph of the Dobson's beloved dog, Mitzi. Since I was hoping to surprise Julie with a dog for Christmas, I was curious about the late dog's breed. When Dr. Dobson returned, I began asking him some questions.

"What kind of dog was Mitzi?" I asked, pointing in the direction of the photo.

"You've got me," he replied. "Her daddy was a travelin' man!"

We laughed. "Why do you ask?" he said. "Do you and Julie have a dog?"

"Not yet," I responded, "but we're thinking about it. I've been talking with some Labrador breeders here in town. Do you know of any?"

I should have known better than to ask, having read all of his books. "Paul," he said, "we've always gone down to the pound and found the most forlorn animals and tried to nurse 'em back to health. Mitzi was no different. You should have seen her when she first came to us. We think someone must have beaten her with a shovel; look at how her lip is crooked. Her ribs were protruding. She was in *bad* shape. We took that dog in and let me tell you something: She was the best dog we've ever had!"

Indeed, Proverbs 12:10 speaks to that point: "A righteous

man cares for the needs of his animal, but the kindest acts of the wicked are cruel."

I offer that story at the start of this chapter, not to suggest Jim Dobson as a candidate for president of the ASPCA, but because I think it epitomizes the "care without flair" attitude that I've seen in his office on a daily basis. It is a quality that not only transcends ideological grounds, but one that serves as a foundational principle of the ministry itself.

THE IMAGINARY SIGN

Del Tackett vividly remembers his first day on the job at Focus on the Family. After twenty years in the air force—during which time he rose to the rank of deputy commander of NORAD (North American Aerospace Defense Command) here in Colorado Springs—and a two-year stint as a liaison in the White House under President George H. W. Bush—Del was no stranger to the pressures associated with high expectations. Nonetheless, a meeting with Dr. Dobson that first afternoon at Focus proved memorably poignant. Here is how Del remembers it:

> *At some point in our meeting, Dr. Dobson walked me over to one of the large windows in his office and pointed in the direction of the parking lot. "Del," he began, "imagine if there were 250,000 people standing in that parking lot right now as we speak. Now, imagine if all 250,000 wanted something from you. Would you try and help them all? Of course you would. But what if you let even one or two of them down and they left unsatisfied? Would that be okay? Of course not! You see, those 250,000 people represent all of the phone calls and letters we get every month from people who are in need of something and they're hoping to get it from us. They're trusting us to help them out, and we can't let them down. As you begin your time here, I hope you remember that we have an imaginary sign that's sitting on our front lawn. It reads, "We care about you."*

THE MOST IMPORTANT PERSON IN THE WORLD

As Focus on the Family's vice president of public affairs, Ken Windebank and his team of able representatives spend over ninety days a year traveling on behalf of Dr. Dobson and Don Hodel, thanking the many generous contributors who donate to the ministry. On occasion, Ken and his team will host social events both here in Colorado Springs and at other locations around the country with Dr. and Mrs. Dobson in attendance. These gatherings are great fun and a tremendous source of encouragement to the Dobsons, who love the social interaction that accompanies the get-togethers.

Following a speech or other public event, Dr. and Mrs. Dobson invariably will throw their watches aside and personally meet as many people as they possibly can. They love interacting with listeners and other friends of Focus on the Family even though they're usually exhausted after a long day on the road. But these meet and greets are not cut from the same cloth as a political rope line, in which the figure is simply interested in pressing the flesh to get credit for the visit.

Ken explains: "It is an amazing thing to watch. Dr. Dobson will never look over your shoulder while talking with you, hoping to spy someone more important to spend his time with. He looks you in the eye and cares to hear what you have to say. When you're talking with Dr. James Dobson, you're the most important person in the world to him at that very moment."

Del Tackett echoes those sentiments. "If you're at a meeting with Jim Dobson, he'll never give you one of those nonverbal responses, like an eye roll or a sigh that says, 'I've had enough.' So gracious is the man that even if a story you're telling is long, he'll sometimes ask you a question that will make it longer, simply because he cares to know!"

James Dobson's outward expressions of love and attention aren't reserved for fellow employees or constituents of Focus on the Family. As he travels, he regularly meets people who may be marginally familiar with his radio program or who simply recall seeing him on television. "He'll always give them as much time as his schedule will allow," says security chief Bruce Hoover. "He'll never brush someone off for the sake of convenience." On occasion, Dr. Dobson comes home with a name and address of one of those people, and he'll do his best to send some practical help their way in the form of a check, book, or tape. Rather than just shake a hand, the man does his best to show Christ's love through his actions as well as his words.

"HOLEY" ROLLER

From the beginning of his ministry, Dr. Dobson has always been more concerned with being faithful to the mission of the organization than with trying to impress his audience. Paul Hetrick tells of a meeting he attended with Dr. Dobson and Word executives back in the 1980s regarding the Turn Your Hearts toward Home film series.

As Paul remembers, they were in the midst of a brainstorming session and Dr. Dobson, as was his custom, was writing feverishly on the blackboard in the front of the room. Because he was moving so quickly, he had taken off his shoes to increase both his comfort and his agility on the carpeted floor. After he ran out of room on the board, he continued his note taking on large, white sheets of paper. As he was kneeling down on the ground to tape the strategy sheets to the wall, Paul noticed that Dr. Dobson—the best-selling author and psychologist who had been seen by more than 50 million people on film—was toiling away with holes in his socks, in clear view of the room full of people. In modern lingo, we'd call that being "too cool to care"—that is, too cool to care what other people think.

At that moment, Paul says, he was reminded once again that Dr. James Dobson doesn't care much about impressing people—he simply cares about doing what needs to be done.

THE SUBTLETIES THAT GO UNSEEN

The apostle Paul urged the Colossians that they should clothe themselves with "compassion, kindness, humility, gentleness and patience" (Colossians 3:12). When you boil this principle down to its core, that's exactly what "forget the flair—just care" is about. It's about forgoing your own comfort for the sake of the other guy. It's thinking about yourself less and about others more.

Dale Carnegie, the public speaking and personality development pioneer of the early 1900s, summed it up perfectly: "Do things for others and you'll find your self-consciousness evaporating like morning dew on a Missouri cornfield in July." This is exactly the approach that Dr. Dobson takes. Being close to Dr. Dobson on a daily basis, I often see how he expresses his care for others in terms of dollars and cents. But I'd rather tell you about the things that go unseen. James Dobson's propensity to care without flair is exhibited in the *invisible* check that's seen in the subtle sacrifice of his time and talents.

SURPRISE VISITS

Just three months into my first job at Focus, my colleague and cubicle neighbor John Klotz suffered a heart attack while sitting at his desk. By God's grace, John survived and returned to work only a few weeks later. When I called John shortly after the incident, he told me rather nonchalantly that Dr. Dobson had paid him a visit his second night in the hospital.

A few months later, I heard of another ailing employee who had been visited by the boss at the hospital downtown. *How neat,* I thought, *that given his busy schedule, he makes these types of visits a priority.* The pattern has continued ever since, though Dr. Dobson hardly ever talks about it and actually would find it odd that people are surprised by his visits to a hurting fellow staff member.

TUGGING ON THE HEART, NOT TOOTING ON A HORN

"'Umble we are, 'umble we have been, 'umble we shall ever be," said Mrs. Heep in the Charles Dickens classic *David Copperfield*—and so it is at Focus on the Family because of Dr. James Dobson's demand for humility in all endeavors. *No brag, no swag*—that's the silent motto within the office walls of James Dobson.

Let's put a wrap on this principle with a good joke that Jim Dobson's been known to tell from time to time. Since humor can sometimes drill home a point that a literal account might otherwise miss, I think you'll see the message woven within the irony. At the onset, I should remind you that this is pure fiction—and that any resemblance to real life is purely coincidental!

As the story goes, Dr. Dobson's secretary, Sherry Hoover, received a phone call that went something like this:

Caller: I'd like to speak to the top dog at Focus on the Family.

Sherry: Sir, are you asking to talk to the chairman?

Caller: I don't care what you call him; I want to talk to the top dog.

At this point, Sherry begins to get a little irritated.

Sherry: We have no dogs here, sir . . . only people. I'm sorry, but you'll have to be more specific about who you want.

Caller: Well, as you will. I just want to tell the top dog that I want to give five million dollars to Focus on the Family.

At this point, Sherry nearly drops the phone but recovers quickly enough to respond.

Sherry: Oh, wait just a minute! I think I hear Dr. Bowser coming down the hall now.

Of course, the story is just a joke, but I can assure you that at Focus on the Family this exchange would never happen, because every single call is treated with the same level of care and concern regardless of who might be on the other end, what they may want, or what they may want to give.

When you care without the flair, compassion, kindness, humility, gentleness, and patience will surely accompany the effort.

POINTS TO REMEMBER

★ When you humble yourself to the service of others, offering comfort and care becomes a powerful privilege as opposed to simply a burden to bear.

★ If you're taking the time to talk with someone, take the time to commit your full attention to the conversation. Treat them as if they were the most important person in the world to you, because at that moment they should be.

★ Sincerity is a subtle characteristic, revealed not only in what you do, but also in the way you get something done.

★ If God sees everyone as equal in *His* eyes, why should we see anyone differently? Concern yourself with caring for others and the Lord will take good care of you.

PRACTICAL PRINCIPLE #14

DO WHAT'S RIGHT—
ENDURE THE FIGHT

*It's a little like wrestling a gorilla. You don't
quit when you're tired—you quit when
the gorilla is tired.*
ROBERT STRAUSS

We arrive now at the principle that generates the single greatest concentration of publicity in the life of Dr. James Dobson. By living according to this simple code of conduct—doing the right thing despite the consequences—the man I write about has been vilified and loathed, but also vindicated and loved.

This same child psychologist whose main motive has been to preserve the traditional institution of the family has journeyed through both storm and sunshine over the course of nearly forty years in public life. He is an anomaly, because unlike leaders whose feet sit in shifting sand, James Dobson stands for something—regardless of the price or the pain he may endure in the process.

Consider some of the bombastic charges lobbed against him and things he has been called in recent years:

- "a guy who would smack you down if you gave him any lip"
- "the Godzilla of the right"
- "preacher politician"
- "religious right power broker"
- a man who operates "a radio-driven theocratic crusade"

Incidentally, this sampling of comments come from just one man: *New York Times* columnist Frank Rich. Mr. Rich has made a career of attacking the conservative beliefs of Christians who have the guts to take an unpopular but moral stand in the culture. Unfortunately, he is hardly alone. As an assistant to Dr. Dobson, I sort through piles of similarly worded assaults each week. To be honest, I think those of us on staff get more agitated about the personal attacks on our boss than the boss does himself. During a recent address to the National Religious Broadcasters Convention, Dr. Dobson spoke to that point. Here is what he said that evening:

> *It is unpleasant to be called "the religious right" and "the far right" and "religious extremists" and "fundamentalist right-wing crazies." None of us like that. But being ridiculed and marginalized is the price we must pay to defend what we believe. Jesus told us that it would be that way.*
>
> *I can tell you that those of us at Focus on the Family have been subjected to some harsh treatment for the stands we have taken. We've had bloody animal parts brought to our front door. We've had our buildings spray painted. We've had lies told about us in Denver and in Colorado Springs. We've been called "fanatics" and worse. The easiest thing for us to have done would have been to quit. But God has called us to stay in the field to the end of the day, and we will do that for as long as we have breath in our bodies. And I beg you to do the same. How can we remain silent when the next generation hangs in the balance?*

BRACING FOR BATTLE

Enduring persistence is a recurring theme in the life of James Dobson. He understands that the battles that often mean the most are usually those that require the most effort. Often protracted in nature, these battles require both patience and perseverance.

In the current cultural battle for traditional values, victory is often preceded by either defeat or significant disappointment. Whether it's a struggle surrounding the sanctity of life, the advances of medical research, or the preservation of the family itself, Dr. Dobson approaches the challenge like a marathoner pacing himself for the hilly miles ahead.

In addition to embracing the promises of Scripture, he heeds the lessons of history. The portrait of Sir Winston Churchill hangs in his office as a reminder and an encouragement to patiently endure. In the middle of the dark days of Nazi oppression, Churchill found seeds of hope:

> When you feel you cannot continue in your position for another minute, and all that is in human power has been done, that is the moment when the enemy is most exhausted, and when one step forward will give you the fruits of the struggle you have borne.[7]

On more than one occasion, when energy is low and the loneliness that accompanies a staunch stance seems nearly too burdensome to bear, I've seen Dr. Dobson take a big deep breath and say resolutely, "Well, somebody has to speak up, and guess what? It looks like I'm elected!"

EARLY SIGNS

Long before God ever laid the ministry of Focus on the Family on the heart of James Dobson, the Lord was using the young psychologist to make a difference in the lives of young children.

While at the USC School of Medicine and Childrens Hospital

Los Angeles, a young Jim Dobson was working primarily with children who suffered from a metabolic disorder called phenyl-ketonuria, or PKU. A genetic disorder that's characterized by an inability of the body to utilize the essential amino acid phenyl-alanine, the condition can quickly lead to brain damage if it's not identified and treated very early in the child's life. As the director of a study conducted in fifteen major medical centers around the United States, Dr. Dobson's team tested the efficacy of a new diet that ultimately proved successful in treatment. For the first time ever, this type of mental retardation could be prevented! As a re-sult of this and other studies conducted throughout the world, every state now screens newborns for PKU at three days of age.

Now, more than thirty years later, the process leading to these new tests and cures might appear to have been a seamless struggle. Yet, it was anything but simple. The researchers faced doubt, opposition, and outright disagreements. Yet a profes-sional commitment, persistent patience, and a desire to do some-thing remarkable ultimately yielded practical success. So it has been in the life of Dr. James Dobson ever since.

AFTERNOON SETBACK TURNS TO PRIME-TIME PRIZE

Friend and colleague Jim Davis recalls how Dr. Dobson became a public figure seemingly overnight after the publication of his first book, *Dare to Discipline.* "We always knew he was going someplace," recalls Davis. "We were teaching a young married Sunday school together at the Pasadena First Church of the Nazarene in California. In two years, our class grew from 25 to 250 people. And let me tell you something. They weren't coming to hear Jim Davis!"

On the heels of his book's success, James Dobson accepted an invitation to appear on Phil Donahue's nationally televised talk show in Chicago. It turned out to be a disaster. Donahue threw one sucker punch after the other and barely let Dr. Dob-son defend his positions. He left the set feeling like a failure.

Back at the hotel, the ferocious blizzard that raged outside his room seemed like a fitting conclusion to the day. After all, he'd been snowed himself! He thought he had done the right thing. What an opportunity to present God's vision of child rearing to a watching world. How could it have gone so wrong so quickly? He had thought this appearance was a golden opportunity to speak to a diverse audience that otherwise would not be reading Christian literature.

Yet here he sat, feeling like a fool and wondering why the Lord would have allowed His name to be ridiculed and His servant embarrassed so blatantly. In spite of his disappointment, Dr. Dobson would quickly see the seeds of success germinating in the ash heap of failure.

That very afternoon Dr. Dobson met with Doug Mains, owner of the Domain advertising agency, and together they discussed the possibility of a short radio feature dealing with the combined issues of faith and family. A pilot program was recorded and the deal was launched when Tyndale House Publishers agreed to give Dr. Dobson a grant of $35,000 in exchange for the book that later came to be known as *The Strong-Willed Child.* That book has now sold over two million copies. It all started in the ashes of an embarrassing failure on national television. Isn't that a remarkable turn of events? Dr. Dobson did what was right, staying the course even though failure looked like the final outcome, and in the end, God turned his struggle into success. The apostle Paul likewise encouraged the Galatians to persevere in doing what was right. "Let us not become weary in doing good, for at the proper time we will reap a harvest if we do not give up" (Galatians 6:9).

UNWAVERING RESOLVE

If you were to ask close confidants of James Dobson to describe a defining characteristic of their friend, you'd inevitably hear some variation of the qualities associated with passionate perseverance.

"He's a guy who will do what's right no matter the cost," says Ron Wilson, Focus on the Family's vice president of Human Resources. "He will die before he yields."

Jim Davis notes that James Dobson is opinionated but that "his opinions are based on factual truth that's been first vetted by the Word of God."

One of Jim Dobson's favorite quotes is "Millions for defense, but not one cent for tribute." The adage was first coined by U.S. Representative Robert Harper in 1798 in response to France's attempt to blackmail the United States into a 10 million–dollar loan. Indeed, this once rallying cry of a young American nation nicely captures the fervor of the man who believes, as did Abraham Lincoln, that "right makes might."

In terms of integrity and character, Dr. Dobson views compromise of character and commitment as akin to cowardice. If you were to ask him how long you must endure the hardships associated with doing the right thing at the right time, his answer, in the form of a question, would be, How high is up?

SITTING ON THE SIDE OF TRUTH

Of all the battles raging across the cultural war front today, the thirty-year fight on behalf of the unborn baby seems to hold the greatest hope for success. Back when Dr. Dobson first began Focus on the Family, abortionists used to hide behind the mysteries associated with the timing of conception and infant viability. Radical feminists told the nation that unborn children were just "meaningless protoplasm" and "a blob of tissue."

Technology has made them look ridiculous. We now know that a child's heart begins to beat at eighteen to twenty-one days after fertilization; after eight weeks all body systems are present; and by the twelfth week, the baby's fingerprints have begun forming! To those determined to murder preborn children at will, these facts have become the enemy of their cause.

Over the course of the debate, James Dobson hasn't yielded

despite the arrows and attacks from the other side. Science continues to prove this belief correct. Tenacity, patience, prayer—and technology—serve as pro-life's greatest weapons as the fight moves forward. In December of 2003, Dr. Dobson and I were discussing the upcoming January letter detailing this very subject. There was optimism in the air as we discussed the recently passed ban on partial-birth abortion.

As we concluded, Dr. Dobson looked at me squarely and said something I'll never forget. "Paul," he said, "isn't it good to be on the side of truth? If we stay the course, our positions will never contradict themselves. We may not win every battle, but we will ultimately win every war."

CONCLUDING THOUGHTS

On the eve of a Focus on the Family board meeting in February 2004, James Dobson worked late into the night on a report he entitled "The State of the Family." With the prospect of gay marriage looming and judges ignoring both the law and the will of the people, the culture appeared to be approaching a critical crossroads. Through campaign finance reform, the Internal Revenue Service and Congress were trying to stifle the Christian and conservative views of nonprofit organizations like Focus on the Family. Here is a portion of what Dr. Dobson shared with his advisors as they convened on campus the next day:

Throughout the Scriptures, God's people were instructed to put everything on the line to accomplish His purposes. Esther and Gideon and David and Elijah and Moses and Paul and Barnabas and Peter and Silas and James all acted in opposition to the established law of their time. The apostles and disciples suffered for their civil disobedience with imprisonment and eventual execution. Our founding fathers also risked their lives in the pursuit of freedom. Are we now going to withdraw from the fray because of an oppressive government that threatens to destroy us? I pray not.

His prayer has been answered. With a unified board and an energized staff committed to the battle, Dr. Dobson exudes a confident and contagious spirit.

In Charles Dickens's classic work *Great Expectations,* you might recall a young orphan boy named Philip Pirrip, or Pip for short. Pip was poor and struggling and could only fantasize about one day becoming a man of great worth and significant character. Yet despite his grandest dreams, how far could an orphan of his era expect to go? If you know the story, you'll remember that a London lawyer named Mr. Jaggers finds Pip and gives him astonishing news: An unknown benefactor has bequeathed him a fortune! Says the lawyer to the young Pip, "My boy, you have great expectations."

Likewise for the person who does the right thing despite the price he must pay in the process. In every endeavor, endure the fight—do what's right—and good things will eventually happen (even if we don't see the results during our lifetime) because "at the proper time we will reap a harvest if we do not give up" (Galatians 6:9).

POINTS TO REMEMBER

★ "By standing firm you will gain life" (Luke 21:19).

★ In failure you can find the seeds of future success.

★ "You need to persevere so that when you have done the will of God, you will receive what he has promised" (Hebrew 10:36).

★ Truth will never tease or toy with you; truth will never contradict fact. "Since you have kept my command to endure patiently, I will also keep you from the hour of trial that is going to come upon the whole world to test those who live on the earth" (Revelation 3:10).

PRACTICAL PRINCIPLE #15

MAKE A FRIEND

Am I not destroying my enemies when
I make friends of them?
Abraham Lincoln

For most, it was a stunning sight to see.

After two long years of rancorous debate and exhaustive investigation, the nine-member panel of the National Gambling Impact Study Commission had just concluded its final meeting. From the first gathering in 1997 to the final day on June 3, 1999, Dr. James Dobson had gone toe-to-toe with several members of the panel, but none more so than J. Terrence Lanni.

Their sharp and sometimes heated exchanges throughout the previous two years of testimony and discussion had been widely covered by the press. As the chairman of the board and CEO of MGM Grand, Inc. (an entertainment, hotel, and gaming company headquartered in Las Vegas), Mr. Lanni's support for gambling was the polar opposite of Jim Dobson's long-held belief that the industry was preying on the poor and causing irreparable harm to families in the process. To the casual observer, there was obviously no love lost between the two men.

Yet when the gavel dropped, J. Terrence Lanni, the same man who had opposed James Dobson throughout the process, jumped to his feet and embraced him with the kind of warmth reserved for a good friend. Those marginally familiar with Jim Dobson were shocked. Those who knew him well were not.

Mike Benzie, manager of security at Focus on the Family, had traveled with Dr. Dobson to all twenty-four of the commission's meetings in various cities around the country. While most of the events seemed to blend one into the other, a trip to San Diego and the Santa Anita racetrack was memorable for Mike. The situation speaks well to James Dobson's penchant for making believers out of skeptics and eliciting respect from those who stand in stark ideological disagreement with him.

As Mike recalls, the meeting, which was open to the public, was packed with vocal union employees of the racetrack. "They were ready for a fuss and a fight," remembers Mike. "They had protest signs plastered all over. The crowd was far from friendly."

But as the proceedings got under way, Dr. Dobson spoke directly to the hostile audience. While no tape is available of the discussion, this is the essence of what he said: "I appreciate your interest in our discussions, and I know that many of you have a very different perspective on this business than do I. But I want you to know something today. We're not here to close you down—I know this is how you make your living— we're simply here to see how gambling affects the family. To that end, your help will be very much appreciated."

According to Mike, those few words completely turned the tenor of the meeting. It was as if water had been poured on the flames. With a cordial demeanor and a direct approach, Dr. Dobson does well in defusing the most combustible of circumstances. He speaks honestly, forthrightly, and directly— but always with a spirit of kindness. By respecting the other person's perspective, James Dobson has made friends with people who don't necessarily share his point of view.

WHEN IDEOLOGIES COLLIDE

A few months ago, we were in the studio preparing for a radio broadcast. Tight on time, Dr. Dobson had rushed down from the third floor and was feverishly making last-minute adjustments to the order of the program. In the midst of his preparations, he was given a note informing him that a group of students from Colorado College had come for a tour of Focus on the Family and were now sitting on the other side of the glass in the gallery. This university is one of the most liberal in the United States, and the students are said to be even more liberal than the professors. "Would you please greet them and answer a few questions?" read the note. Never one to be rude, he agreed.

He opened with a casual greeting and then asked if anyone had questions. Did they ever—except they were actually political statements couched in the form of wild accusations. For the next fifteen minutes, student after student hammered away. "Why do you discriminate against homosexual people who want to marry?" "Why are you opposed to euthanasia; isn't it the humane antidote to pain?" "Why do you want to tell a woman what she can and cannot do with her body?" "Why are you in favor of child abuse—of parents beating and spanking their kids?"

My favorite, however, came from a confused chap who wondered why Dr. Dobson thought widows shouldn't be allowed to marry. Perplexed, my boss asked him where he had heard such a thing. Indignant to the suggestion that he was in error, the male student pointed to a Focus on the Family tour guide and said, "She told us you believe marriage is an eternal bond, even after you die." As it turned out, the fellow had misunderstood and confused the institution of marriage with the promise of salvation!

With each question—or accusation—Dr. Dobson gently yet passionately laid out his position. Sitting in the studio and looking out at the students, I enjoyed watching their reactions to each "controversial" response. Despite their differences, the mood of the room softened the more Dr. Dobson spoke. While he probably didn't change many minds that afternoon, the final tone of the discussion suggested that these students had entered with one assumption and left with another.

That's because when faced with overwhelming opposition, Dr. James Dobson never hides or compromises. He confronts the resistance not with fire or physical fight, but like a winsome warrior who knows the power of his words. His tactics serve as a wonderful blueprint for those who find themselves in tough ideological spots that require gentle diplomacy. In dealing with all confrontation, Dr. Dobson is:

- cordial and respectful in all conversation and discussion;
- bold in the defense of his beliefs;
- empathetic in response to the hurt that regularly accompanies the hostility;
- consistent with the teachings of Scripture.

How, you might ask, does he maintain this decorum even under fire? During a recent discussion in his office, I expressed frustration with the way conservative Christians are depicted in the press these days. The Boy Scouts of America—guilty of hate speech? The Pledge of Allegiance—unconstitutional because it mentions God? How, I wondered, could he maintain this winsome spirit in the midst of relentless opposition? How did he bite his tongue and not just tell off his attackers?

With a smile he raised his index finger and said with assurance, "Ah yes, but 'with him is only the arm of flesh, but with us is the Lord our God to help us and to fight our battles' " (2 Chronicles 32:8). It's this perspective that has allowed Jim Dobson to hold on to hope when the horizon looks bleak. And it's because of this that my boss believes in making friends with people who disagree with him. If you want to make a difference and change hearts and minds to the saving message of Jesus Christ, you first need to forge a relationship with the people who think differently than you do.

HIS FAVORITE LIBERAL

Since 1996, Alan Colmes has been Sean Hannity's liberal counterpart on FOX News Channel's number one program, *Hannity & Colmes*. He is passionate and predictable—and a man whose opinions stand diametrically opposed to those of Dr. James Dobson. Nevertheless, the two men have brokered a friendship over the past few years, warming up to each other personally, if not ideologically.

"Alan's a nice guy," said Dr. Dobson recently. "He's my favorite liberal."

This is the type of comment that may surprise those who see James Dobson as their ideological archenemy, because they weren't expecting to see a man who can respect and befriend someone who disagrees with his opinions on the vast majority of issues.

Just last year, the local chapter of a homosexual organization requested a tour of the Focus on the Family campus to "commemorate" Gay Pride Day. Thirty-five men and women showed up on a Saturday afternoon for the visit and all were cordial and respectful. During a conversation with a guide, one visitor revealed a story that surprised many in the group.

The woman, a self-described lesbian, told of a time a few years earlier when, struggling to make rent, she had contacted Focus on the Family to tell us of her troubles and ask for some advice. The representative she had spoken with arranged for the ministry to pay that particular month's rent, all on her word—and all because she was struggling.

These stories are shared not to suggest that values and

standards are second in importance to a compassionate spirit, but instead to affirm just how seriously Dr. Dobson takes the two greatest commands of Jesus Christ. To the Pharisees Jesus said, "Love the Lord your God with all your heart and with all your soul and with all your mind," and "Love your neighbor as yourself" (Matthew 22:37, 39).

James Dobson urges his staff to put an arm around those who may be hurting, and to offer to help in practical ways.

RAPID RAPPORT

"Dr. Dobson cares about three main things," Don Hodel recently told me, "and those three items are relationships, relationships, and relationships!" Indeed, from my vantage point, it's clear that James Dobson sees every relationship as a *personal* association.

While many professionals draw clear lines between business and private affiliations, Dr. Dobson rarely does. He'll treat a vendor with as much respect and courtesy as he extends to a constituent of Focus or a childhood friend.

First hired as a part-timer eighteen years ago after a game of basketball in the Dobsons' backyard, Gary Lydic sees Dr. Dobson's habit of making friends as simply a way of life. "In the early days, the boss began sending some of us around the country to thank the generous folks who were donating to the ministry," says Gary. "But he didn't just want us to say thanks; he always wanted us to ask another question and that was, 'How can we help *you*?' It was an amazing thing to watch because when a representative from a nonprofit organization shows up to thank you for a gift, you naturally think he's really there to ask for more. People were always waiting for the other shoe to drop . . . and it never would!" With a gleam in his eye, Gary paused, no doubt letting his mind wander back to those initial meetings. Shaking his head, he slapped his hand on the table, and with great emphasis said, "I loved it!"

GUIDING PRINCIPLE

When I was first hired, I became friends with Al DeLaRoche. Al does much of what Gary did—he travels around the country, ministering to families who have expressed some form of interest in the mission of Focus on the Family. Everybody loves Al, and with good reason. He's ambitious, enthusiastic, and committed to the cause of Christ.

At lunch one day, just months after our first meeting, I began quizzing him on the specifics of his job. At the time, I wasn't completely familiar with the philosophy of his department and when I asked him if he minded "raising money," he recoiled at the concept.

"Paul," he said, in an almost fatherly tone, "we're not fundraisers—we're friend-raisers. We simply thank people for their interest and then tell them what God has called us to do. We're about meeting needs, not just making a budget."

THE SECRET BEHIND THE SUCCESS

Have you ever wondered how a man whose exposure is limited to the one-way medium of radio has managed to connect so intimately with millions of people around the world? The answer is simple: by employing the same habits associated with forging new friendships. James Dobson has turned radio—a traditionally passive communicative tool—into a two-way conversation instrument. With every broadcast, the host cares as much about how people respond to the message as he does to the specifics of the message itself. The program is a dialogue with either a guest in the studio or a mother listening in her car. Dr. Dobson constantly solicits a reaction to everything he has to say because he wants to make sure he's meeting the needs of his listeners. Why? In the words of Christian business leader John Maxwell, "People don't care how much you know until they know how much you care."

If you were to go back and review the original Focus on the Family film series, you'd see more than just the changing styles of the times, like wide and wild ties, loud sports jackets, and long sideburns. You would notice that the film follows a very predictable pattern: Dr. Dobson speaks; the camera shows the audience clapping. The host continues speaking; there's a shot of the audience laughing. Dr. Dobson tells a story; the camera shows a woman crying. Why? Is it manipulation? No! The film is a conversation, and that's the way real life happens.

KNOWLEDGE IS THE KEY

To the ignorant, little knowledge seems to lead to firm and certain opinion—however false it may be. Such was the case, said a friend of mine, when attorneys began picking the jury for the case of Kerry S. Dore.

Mr. Dore, a former construction worker who had worked on building the new Focus on the Family offices in the early 1990s, took four employees hostage during a standoff in the lobby of headquarters on May 2, 1996. Allegedly hurt during the construction process, Mr. Dore threatened to blow up the building if Focus officials didn't help him settle his disability dispute with compensation authorities.

Although Mr. Dore was later found guilty of the attack and sentenced to prison, an interesting pattern developed during jury selection that again speaks to Dr. Dobson's ability to—in the words of Dale Carnegie—"win friends and influence people."

As the story goes, our attorney told us that a prospective juror was thought to have a positive view of Focus on the Family, and subsequently James Dobson if one of three scenarios proved true:

1. He or she had either read one of Dr. Dobson's books or heard one of his radio programs.
2. He or she had personally visited the campus of Focus on the Family.
3. He or she personally knew someone who worked at Focus on the Family.

Conversely, if prospective jurors met none of these criteria, they were more likely to hold a negative opinion of both Focus on the Family and Dr. James Dobson himself.

Issues of prospective juror bias notwithstanding, what this reveals is obvious, isn't it? When given the opportunity to interact with the public, Dr. Dobson inevitably connects with them, or at the least earns their respect. He knows how to make friends because he is himself a friendly and authentic man.

SIMPLE KINDNESS

As I write, it occurs to me that some of you might be suspicious of the sincerity behind this principle. Believe me, so was I—until I had the opportunity to see for myself that James Dobson is the real deal. What you see from your view on the outside is the same thing I see from my seat inside Focus on the Family.

In a recent radio commentary, Dr. Dobson described an experience that illustrates this principle of kindness beautifully. With his own words, allow me to share the story:

> *A few years ago I slipped into a market to buy a few groceries for lunch. Standing in front of me at the checkout was an elderly woman who didn't seem to be altogether lucid. It quickly became obvious that she had selected more food than she could pay for as she fumbled in her purse frantically for a few more coins. The checker politely continued to add up the items.*
>
> *"I just don't understand where my money is," said the lady, as she made another desperate foray into the depths of her purse.*
>
> *With that, I whispered to the checker, "Just go ahead and total her bill, then accept whatever money she has and put the rest on my bill."*
>
> *That's what she did, and I paid an extra eight dollars to make up the difference. The old woman never knew that I had helped her. She shuffled off with her cart, relieved that her groceries had cost exactly the amount of money she was able to*

locate. Then I looked back at the checker and saw that she was crying. I asked her why.

"Because," she said, "I've been doing this work for twenty years, and I've never seen anyone do something like that before."

It was no big deal—an insignificant eight dollars—but simple kindness is so unusual today that it shocks us when it occurs. I'll tell you this: That may have been the best eight dollars I ever spent! I only wish I had paid the rest of the dear lady's bill.

James Dobson didn't tell this story for the sake of personal aggrandizement, but in its telling he unknowingly illustrated the substance of the principle in articulate fashion. This principle has a strong foundation: Jesus said, "Give to the one who asks you" (Matthew 5:42) and "Freely you have received, freely give" (Matthew 10:8).

POINTS TO REMEMBER

★ Making a friend is not always about finding someone just like yourself. The relationships that can make the greatest difference are those in which the friends differ most.

★ Although the process might take more time, the winsome warrior often accomplishes far more than the bombastic battler.

★ Treat every relationship as a personal friendship and the person on the receiving end is more likely to reciprocate in kind.

★ Respect precedes sincerity, and sincerity assures respect.

PRACTICAL PRINCIPLE #16

GOOD MANNERS MATTER

Young gentleman, we have no printed rules.
We have but one rule here, and it is that every
student must be a gentleman.
ROBERT E. LEE, AS PRESIDENT
OF WASHINGTON COLLEGE

When the schedule permits it, Shirley and Jim Dobson love to take a Saturday night date. After a long week, there's nothing they like better than to have dinner either alone or with friends, and then catch a movie afterwards. (In recent years, they have resorted to videos because so many current movies are filled with profanity, sex, and violence.) Given the daily pressures they encounter and the responsibilities they shoulder, the movie theater provides a much-needed respite and a chance to unplug from the world outside.

Sometimes, that is, but not always.

During the winter of 2003, Joe Kubishta, Shirley Dobson's stepfather, was spending his final days on earth in a California hospital, dying of leukemia at the age of 91. (To read more about this remarkable man, log on to the Focus on the Family Web site at http://family.org/docstudy/newsletters/a0025500.cfm.) For several months, the Dobsons had shuttled back and forth from Colorado to California, each time expecting that their visit with Joe would be their last. Back home in Colorado Springs, they knew that each phone call from California could carry the news nobody wanted to hear. It was a somber season in the Dobson household, however resigned they were to the inevitable passing of their beloved Joe.

During this time, Shirley and Jim Dobson decided to take a break and go see a movie. Arriving to a nearly full showing just as the lights were beginning to go down, they found their way to the very last row in the back of the theater and stumbled across a dozen irritated people before finally settling into their seats. It was a bad way to begin a good movie.

It actually got worse.

About halfway into the movie, the piercing ring of a cell phone collided with the quiet air. Where was the shrill sound coming from? You guessed it. Shirley Dobson's purse! Worrying that she might miss a call concerning her father, she had brought the phone but mistakenly put it on ring mode rather than vibrate. Heads were turning; people began squirming. A revolt was imminent! Hoping to stave off the insurrection, Shirley dug deep into her bag and tried to find the phone in the darkness. At last, she found it—but in she couldn't see the buttons. It continued to ring loudly while Shirley frantically punched at the phone. By this time, people within twenty feet in all directions were livid. Dr. Dobson says they would have killed if they could have gotten their hands on them. The guy sitting directly in front of them was especially angry, turning sideways and sighing and huffing to show his irritation. Meanwhile, the phone continued to ring. Finally, the Dobsons stood and began tripping over the people in the row once more. Indeed, the call was from Shirley's brother, but the news was simply an update. They returned to the theater and, of course, stepped over the same dozen folks en route to their seats. Embarrassed and wrung out by that point, they sat down to watch the rest of the movie.

When the lights came on, Dr. Dobson thought he should

apologize to the irritated man in front of them and explain that Shirley's father was dying—which is why the phone was on in the first place. The disgruntled man turned around as Jim Dobson began to speak. "Sir, I'm really sorry about the phone . . ." But at that point he was shocked to realize that the man was from Focus on the Family! They actually worked together in producing the radio broadcast. Dr. Dobson was saying, "I'm so sorry . . ." and the man was saying with great sincerity, "I am sooo sorry . . ." It was an awkward moment that brought much laughter afterwards.

When Dr. Dobson tells the story now, he adds, "So, I fired him." Not true. They had fun telling about it the next day.

A TELLING TALE

I share that story for a variety of reasons. First, for its sheer irony, especially given the long odds of the Dobsons sitting directly behind an employee in a town of over half a million people. Second, because our values and standards are often best exposed or revealed during the onset of adverse circumstances, this incident speaks volumes to the character of the couple.

For those of us who know the Dobsons personally, they are the last people we'd expect to see raising a ruckus in the middle of a movie! Most telling is not how or why the action unfolded, it's how they reacted to the gaffe itself: with a spirit of concerted and conciliatory humility.

Dr. Dobson believes that good manners are not only a sign of civility, but also a measure befitting the conduct of someone who knows Jesus Christ. As Paul urged Titus, we're "to slander no one," but instead to "be peaceable and considerate, and to show true humility toward all men" (Titus 3:2). This is not always an easy charge to keep, but it's a code that Dr. Dobson takes very seriously. "He has a sense of graciousness and politeness," says Del Tackett, "that's unusual for a man of his position. If I walk into his office, he'll always get up from his desk to greet me, offer a smile, and shake my hand. Always kind. Always well-mannered. That's Dr. James Dobson."

As someone who walks in and out of his office dozens of times per day, I can confirm this. No matter how busy or burdened the man may be, every assignment he gives is first prefaced with a please and acknowledged with a thank-you upon completion of the task. It may seem to be a minor touch, but I assure you, it's a gesture that goes a long way.

THE SLIPPERY SLOPE

A major study conducted by the North American etiquette companies found that 80 percent of Americans polled thought rudeness in business was on the rise. Perhaps even more telling, however, was a follow-up question. Of those who encountered rude behavior, 58 percent reported that they immediately took their business elsewhere "regardless of cost or inconvenience."[8]

Imagine what that's doing to the bottom line for the worst offenders. I suspect this reaction is applicable and relevant to all types of industry in this country, ministry included. That's why over twenty-seven years ago, Dr. Dobson laid out the standards of professional conduct for his employees. Upon hire, every Focus on the Family representative is reminded that responding with what Dr. Dobson calls a "personal touch" is not only recommended—it's required. Here is his reasoning:

> We claim to be Christians who care about people. If we are rude or discourteous to them, we contradict our witness and appear as phonies. For some, we even undermine their belief in Jesus because we as His representatives are so uncaring.

According to that mission statement, it's clear that good manners go far beyond obeying simple rules of etiquette. This

all-encompassing quality affects many aspects of personal behavior. If you were to visit the campus of Focus on the Family
or contact us by telephone, you would note several significant,
though perhaps subtle, indications of this truth:

- **Dress Code:** Employees dress both modestly and
  professionally. Men wear slacks and neckties; women
  wear skirts and dresses. If friends of the ministry make
  the effort to visit, employees will show them respect
  by dressing in a sharp and honorable manner.
- **Salutations:** Correspondence is addressed accordingly.
  Rather than resorting to first-name familiarity, you'll
  find "Mr." or "Mrs." or "Miss" on each letter or package. Phone representatives refer to callers in the same
  way. This is not a reflection of stuffiness, but an
  extension of due deference.
- **Phone Etiquette:** As noted earlier, every call is to be
  picked up by the third ring if possible. Furthermore,
  if you try to call someone directly at Focus on the
  Family, you'll always talk with a real person because
  phones are not permitted to roll directly to voice mail.
  As if to punctuate his belief in the personal touch, Dr.
  Dobson's office remains the last holdout of voice mail
  altogether. Our messages arrive on paper or by e-mail,
  not via a blinking bulb on the top of the phone. There
  is no "menu" of options for callers to sort through.
  There will never be an automated response, as long
  as Dr. Dobson has his way.

R-E-S-P-E-C-T

These are but a few qualities that extend from the standards of
the man himself. While this is a ministry of 1,300 unique people, the fingerprint of its founder can be lifted from every corner of campus. "Jim Dobson has always insisted that we extend

'world-class hospitality' to those people who cross our path,"
says Ron Wilson. Few would doubt the veracity of that charge.

Executive vice president Diane Passno shares a similar perspective. "Jim Dobson is a southern gentleman," she says. "He
treats women especially beautifully, extending to them the
utmost respect. There was a time when I was the lone woman
on the executive cabinet and you know what? He would stand
when I entered the room and pull my chair out for me before I
sat down."

But it's not just women who receive this level of treatment.
Patty Watkins, a former assistant who now works for Don
Hodel, remarked recently how Dr. Dobson always politely asks if
he might swing into the president's office for a brief question. After all, surmises Patty, he's the chairman of the board. He could
very easily breeze by an assistant without comment or query, but
that's not how he operates. He respects Don's schedule, even
though Don would tell you that James Dobson could have every
minute of it, if he so desired.

FINAL THOUGHTS ON MANNERS

In my capacity, I often have the privilege of sorting through
some of the huge volumes of personal mail that comes across
my boss's desk. To expedite his handling of correspondence,
we'll sort letters and do our best to prioritize them according to
need and relationship. Just before Christmas 2003, a colleague
of mine, John Klotz, sent a friendly note of thanks to Dr. Dobson on the occasion of his twentieth anniversary at Focus on the
Family:

> DR. DOBSON:
> Coming to work for Focus on the Family was the best
> Christmas present I've ever received. I remember the first
> Christmas chapel I attended in December 1983. A well-
> dressed gentleman with sideburns and a wide tie ap-

proached me, gave me a big smile, shook my hand, and said, "Are you John? I'm Jim Dobson—welcome to Focus on the Family!" *How friendly and unassuming,* I thought. Even though I'd only been with Focus for a week or so, I was given a bonus check with everyone else.

Two decades later, the memory still burns brightly in John's mind, serving as a source of encouragement and reminding him that his efforts are well placed and his commitment is appreciated.

As we conclude our discussion on the importance of good manners, I suggest that it's time we take stock of not only the caliber of our conversations, but also the quality of our behavior toward each other. What a powerful and effective witness is the well-mannered individual. Allow your language and actions to serve as your signature throughout society. Be gracious; be guarded; but be gentle. After all, it is courtesy that gives color and character to our lives. It is the essence of good taste—the defining characteristic of a civil world.

POINTS TO REMEMBER

★ Good manners will get you further in life than will good intentions.

★ Civility isn't a suggestion for a Christian; it's a behavioral conviction that we're called to keep.

★ Chivalry is a timeless tenet that will never go out of style.

PRACTICAL PRINCIPLE #17

LEARN TO LAUGH

A sense of humor is part of the art
of leadership, of getting along with people,
of getting things done.
PRESIDENT DWIGHT D. EISENHOWER

Focus on the Family security specialist Den Patterson, a former deputy sheriff from Buena Vista, Colorado, is not the easily flappable sort. With a confident and deliberate stride reminiscent of a lawman from the Wild West, Den has been known to evoke guilt in even the innocent man, all in the name of good fun.

I speak from personal experience. On numerous occasions, the barrel-chested bone crusher has backed me into a corner and questioned my movements around the building. What am I carrying in my hand? Why am I leaving campus at 4 PM? Did I get permission? Does my boss know? The jabs are constant but comical, once you've gotten to know him. He's a good-natured fellow who does his job well and is appreciated and loved by the Dobsons, even though he fills his free time picking on colleagues like me!

However beloved he may be, a crack in Den's demeanor developed late one afternoon upon being summoned to Dr.

Dobson's office. Den says, "I remember thinking, *Oh boy, what have I done now? Is the pink slip on its way?*" A bit shaken, he proceeded to the third floor and was escorted into the library. His palms were sweaty. His heart began to race. Peering in through the doorway, he could see the boss intensely plowing through a stack of reports and letters.

"Please come in, Den," a reserved and serious Jim Dobson began, looking up from his work. "Please have a seat."

Apprehensively, Den slid into the wood-backed chair on the opposite side of the long table.

"We have a situation," began Dr. Dobson, pausing as he looked at a piece of paper and an envelope, "and I'm going to have to ask you a few questions. Are you okay with that?"

"Yes, sir," replied Den.

"I'm just going to need a straight answer," he cautioned. "Please, just answer the question."

Again, Den nodded.

"Den," he began, "I've been hearing from several sources that . . . that you like that sissy game of hockey. Is that correct?"

The swagger began returning in the form of a smile.

"Yes, sir, absolutely!" answered Den. "Why do you ask?"

"Well," Dr. Dobson replied, "I was just wondering if you'd want these two tickets I have to game five of the Stanley Cup finals between the Avalanche and the Detroit Red Wings?"

Of course, Den gratefully accepted, but in pure Den Patterson fashion, he now says, "It was the worst game I ever saw—and I remind him every time I get the chance!"

THE HABIT AND BENEFITS OF HUMOR

Nobody appreciates a good joke or a funny story more than James Dobson. He regularly pulls pranks like the one mentioned above, and gets a good laugh as the target sweats, awaiting the delivery of the punch line. He knows that humor is the salt that adds flavor to life. Like the melody of well-composed music, it brings joy and pleasure, reduces stress, and helps James Dobson to put both the world's and his own personal activities in proper perspective.

Unlike many in modern culture, however, Dr. Dobson's taste for humor is cleaner than a bar of Ivory soap. No one has ever heard him tell an off-color joke—because he's never done it! Indeed, his clean and clever wit serves as a wonderful weapon that helps him cope with the inevitable disappointments that are simply a part of everyday living.

The value he places on humor is legitimate, especially considering the added health benefits that laughter has been proven to provide. Once again, science has confirmed the truth of Scripture. "A happy heart makes the face cheerful, but heartache crushes the spirit," wrote Solomon in Proverbs 15:13. Scientists now suggest that laughter improves such vital functions as heart rate, respiratory rate, and blood pressure. In fact, a good chuckle changes blood chemistry and improves immunity. Have you ever laughed yourself to tears? Even better! A tear from laughter is said to contain a greater concentration of proteins than a tear resulting from an allergic reaction—thus producing a greater flush of poisons from the body.

Interestingly, new research out of the College of William and Mary also suggests that our perception of humor provides a good workout opportunity for the brain. While we normally analyze information in the left cerebral hemisphere, it's the right hemisphere that processes humor. "It's this activity between the two halves of our brains," says Dr. Ravinder Mamtani, a professor of clinical preventative medicine at New York Medical College, "that allows us to get in touch with the lighter side of life, offering alternative perceptions of life situations and ourselves."[9]

Therefore, if you can find humor in even the simplest of circumstances, it's an exercise well worth the effort!

BEYOND THE BENEFITS

However rich the rewards of comic relief may be, the benefits of laughter are a mere afterthought for Dr. Dobson. For him, it's instinctual. While some hard-driving professionals might view humor in the office as an unprofessional interruption, my boss actually sees it as a necessary and natural ingredient to success.

Shortly after coming to work in the chairman's office, I was having lunch with a few of my colleagues when the subject of our favorite foods came up. "Egg salad!" someone enthusiastically shouted out. Dr. Dobson rolled his eyes. "Ugh," he muttered, "not on your life." Gail Hinson, our department's receptionist, asked why.

"Are you concerned about the cholesterol?" she wondered.

"No," he replied, "I just don't like eggs."

"Why?" someone pressed.

He paused.

"Well," he began, "you see, it's like this. When I was about four years old, I figured out where eggs came from—and I decided from then on, that I wasn't going to eat eggs or anything that reminds me of them!"

"Even mayonnaise?" I asked.

"*Especially* mayonnaise," he answered.

Well, apparently word of his aversion to eggs made its way to some of the senior staff, because during an off-site meeting, the dessert one night was vanilla ice cream in big bowls.

But what, you might ask, does vanilla ice cream have to do with eggs?

Not much, except that while everyone at the table was served three scoops of ice cream, Dr. Dobson was served large scoops of mayonnaise! He ate a spoonful, dripping with chocolate sauce, before gagging on the hated stuff. The pranksters were secretly watching from the wings, and they howled with delight when Dr. Dobson plowed into the dessert and made a face.

Illustrative of the good sport he is, and loving a good prank as much as the next guy, he laughed as hard as anyone else around the table—but he still won't eat eggs or anything having to do with them!

Of course, there is a time for sobriety, but what a magnificent thing a sprinkle of laughter is during the tension of the day. For Dr. James Dobson, finding humor—even at his own expense—is a tactic that has not only saved his sanity on occasion, but also offered those of us who work for him a worthy example to follow.

TECHNOLOGY TROUBLES

Would you believe that until 1992, Dr. Dobson wrote every one of his books on yellow notepad paper? It's true! In a world teeming with technological conveniences, it's hard to fathom writing a book with a mere pen and paper, but that's exactly what he did. After he was finished writing, he'd tape the pages together and roll up the manuscript like a scroll. The paper was then handed to a secretary, and the manuscript would be transcribed.

Karen Bethany, who worked for Dr. Dobson for nine years as his executive assistant, remembers when the subject of a computer was first broached. She recalls wondering if he even knew how to type or if the change in routine might prove too distracting. Apprehensively, she approached him and was pleasantly surprised with the reaction she received. While concerned that he hadn't typed in over fifteen years, he was eager to give it a shot. Although it took a bit of getting used to, it took only a weekend before Dr. Dobson was writing all his books on the computer.

Despite a level of comfort with using the computer for word processing, Dr. Dobson was reluctant to delve into the World Wide Web and begin using e-mail. "Paul," he told me on more than one occasion, "that Internet is a black hole—once I get in and start reading, I'll never get out!" Well, after putting up a valiant resistance, he finally succumbed to electronic correspondence early last summer, just prior to departing for a writing trip in London.

Given the seven-hour time difference between Colorado Springs and London and the complexities and costs associated with international facsimiles, the London trip provided a perfect opportunity to break the boss in with e-mail. Those of us on staff were excited about the prospect, because with e-mail, nothing would have to be retyped and there would be no risk of losing a critical document. After a few rounds of early success, things went south—fast.

Patty Watkins arrived to work on the morning of June 10, 2003, and found an e-mail waiting for her from Dr. Dobson. After explaining the many troubleshooting steps he had taken to no avail, he made the following conclusion:

> Patty: Questions . . . Did I just dream that you and Steve e-mailed me last night? (This morning as I write.) Why did my Mac "eat" my messages? Why does it hate me? What did I do to deserve this? Whatever happened to the old-fashioned yellow pads and fax machines? Never have I had a yellow note consume itself and then hide the pieces. I hate the 21st century!! I'm going back to Andy Taylor, Barney Fife, and the warm, friendly town of Mayberry. At least there you could get a great piece of apple pie from Aunt Bea. I haven't had a piece of anybody's apple pie since I got to London—nothing but cursed "sticky buns," that are colorful and look inviting, but have no sugar and taste like cardboard. Strudel is a poor excuse for dessert. And now this computer has run off with my messages and won't play by the rules. What a way to start the day!
>
>   JCD

If laughter is the hand of God on the shoulder of a troubled world, then indeed, the Lord has had his hand on James Dobson his entire life. Like the bald eagle who rides the winds until they carry him high above the storm into the sunshine, my boss has a penchant for finding the humor in almost every circumstance. For fun and maybe just for a break from the business applicability of these principles, let's take a look at the following rather eclectic mix of hilarity, all somehow related to James Dobson.

- **Circa 1945:** Jim Dobson and H. B. London were twelve years old when their families met for a vacation in Santa Fe, New Mexico. One morning, the two of them went golfing. It was very hot, and before long the two boys became thirsty. A sprinkler system seemed very inviting, and they tanked up on water before they saw a sign that warned against drinking it. Wondering what they had done, they asked a groundskeeper what was wrong with the water. "Oh," he said, "it's just distilled sewer water." They went back to the hotel and told their parents what they had done. The boys were taken to a doctor in town, who prescribed a pint of laxative to each to "clear them out." It made them violently sick. They both had terrible diarrhea and for three days silently passed each other coming and going to and from the bathroom. Then they became dehydrated and began vomiting. The Dobson and London families laughed about the episode later, but Jim and H. B. didn't think it was so funny. Neither of them played golf again until they were grown.
- **Circa 1970:** While skiing for an entire day at the Heavenly Valley Ski Resort in Lake Tahoe, James Dobson and Jim Davis began skiing down to the lodge, trying to get in one final fast run. Jim Davis came first, and as he did, he spied a fellow near the bottom of the mountain in an orange vest. He was waving a flag to warn them of a fifty-foot wide by two-foot deep puddle

of melted snow looming large before them. Davis stopped in time. Dr. Dobson didn't—and he careened into the lake at about 30 mph. "He water-skied for about ten feet and then took a giant face plant," remembers Davis, "and was just motionless in the water. Afraid that he was drowning, I dove in and yanked his head up, only to see a guy laughing his head off *at me*. He had been faking it! You know what he said? 'Hey, if I'm going to be wet, you're going to be wet too!'"

- **Circa 1985:** During a thrice-weekly game of basketball held regularly in the Dobson's backyard, the battle of the heavyweights got the best of an innocent garage door one early morning. Once again, the 6'5", 220-pound Jim Davis, who had been an all-American basketball player in college, was in the middle of the trouble, but this time he had a different accomplice. Roger Bowlin, 6'4", a former all-American at the University of Washington, went head-to-head with Jim on a drive to the basket. Bowlin lowered his head, but Davis threw a forearm shiver to his chin—propelling 485 pounds of sloppy sweat into the wooden garage door right beneath the basket. "We completely splintered that door in two!" laughs Jim Davis. "And you know what Dobson did? First, he laughed, than he made me pay for it, fix it, and paint it myself!"

- **Circa 1997:** During a trip for the gambling commission, Dr. Dobson and crew encountered a raging hurricane in New Orleans. The city was flooded and most of the streets were impassable. As security manager Mike Benzie began navigating their vehicle through the flood waters en route to the airport, he heard Dr. Dobson opening and closing the door directly behind him. "What's going on back there?" queried Mike. Dr. Dobson responded, "Hey, I'm just checking. In case we hit really deep water, I'm outta' here!"

THE PUNCH LINE

Levity in life is important, regardless of how onerous one's burdens may be. Jim Dobson realizes this. While it's often far easier to find the humor in a trial whose season has passed, it's nevertheless worthwhile to look for a redeeming quality in the form of jocularity and good fun. The next time you're about ready to hit the roof in frustration, pause and ask yourself this question: *Is there anything remotely funny about this?*

If history is any judge, you might be surprised at what you find!

POINTS TO REMEMBER

★ "A cheerful heart is good medicine, but a broken spirit saps a person's strength" (Proverbs 17:22, NLT).

★ Scientists suggest that every human has five senses: smell, sound, sight, taste, and touch. The successful share two additional ones—common sense and humor!

★ "There is a time for everything . . . a time to laugh" (Ecclesiastes 3:1, 4).

★ A good joke is often more effective than the most compelling argument.

PRACTICAL PRINCIPLE #18

WATCH THE CLOCK—TIMING IS ESSENTIAL

Time goes, you say? Ah, no!
Alas, time stays, we go.
HENRY AUSTIN DOBSON

My office at Focus on the Family is positioned diagonally from Dr. Dobson's and directly opposite the boardroom where both internal and external groups gather to meet with either the chairman or other high-level leaders. It's a good location for a researcher because it enables me to keep my finger on the pulse of the organization through sight, sound, and conversation.

Although I don't have the opportunity or the need to attend every meeting, I've learned a very valuable lesson of life just by sitting at my desk and listening. Listening, that is, not to privileged or private information, but to both the silence and the simple sounds that erupt from behind closed doors.

With a schedule that's packed from morning until night, you'll rarely find Jim Dobson sitting around at a meeting, just waiting for it to begin. On some occasions, he'll swing by for a brief visit, ask or answer questions, and then quickly be on his way. Surely this is not unlike most executives, but from my desk, I've been able to see a predictable pattern that aptly illustrates a critical characteristic of every leader: impeccable timing.

You see, when Dr. Dobson first enters and sits down, I inevitably hear the murmur of reactive and responsive laughter to his opening remarks. Why? He always begins with a light tone and quickly connects with his audience—and they with him. As the meeting progresses, a hush often falls over the group, perhaps indicative of contemplation rather than slumber! As the meeting comes to an end, I can almost perfectly predict when the double door will swing open: just after the laughter and applause. Dr. Dobson isn't one to belabor a point or deliberately drone. He knows when to arrive, how long to stay—and yes, when to leave. To James Dobson, good timing is the ribbon that ties good content together.

A BAD EXAMPLE

Professional athletes should know a thing or two about good timing, but all too often, the lure of past glory and a desire for affirmation and adulation seems to cloud otherwise good judgment about when to leave.

The Great Bambino, Babe Ruth, batted an embarrassing .181 in his final abbreviated season with the Boston Braves. Hall of Fame pitcher Steve Carlton didn't know when to quit either, but it took him two full seasons and an atrocious record of fifteen wins and twenty-eight losses on five separate teams to finally decide it was time to pull the plug. The greatest fighter who ever lived, Muhammad Ali, was beaten by "a bum" at thirty-seven years of age. Following NFL legend Jim Thorpe's final game, a newspaper reporter opined that the man who was voted the greatest athlete of the first half of the twentieth century was "a mere shadow of his former self."[10]

Sadly, an athlete's lack of discretion isn't always limited to the field. At the 2000 Baseball Hall of Fame induction ceremony, Carlton Fisk served up what many have suggested to be the worst sports speech of all time. Over the course of four thousand words, he quoted a Hopi Indian, referred to a man as

"Buddha Boy," and even sent wishes to his grandpa Adolph! The Gettysburg Address it was not. Mistakes like this bring to mind the wonderful yet confused wisdom of another former baseball player, Yogi Berra. "What time is it?" asked a man at the airport. Looking at the traveler with a straight face, Yogi asked innocently, "You mean now?" Indeed, poor timing can tarnish or temper the delivery of otherwise solid material.

If bad timing is considered a pitfall in the sporting world, it can be an absolute disaster in a capitalistic society. Consider just how delicate decisions related to the stock market are these days. A study conducted by a Boston financial research firm discovered that the average investor didn't realize the full benefits of the last bull market (January 1984–December 2000) because of one main miscalculation: bad timing! Despite the fact that the S&P 500 Index returned an average of 16.3 percent a year for the past seventeen years, the average equity investor earned just 5.3 percent a year over the same period of time.[11] Why? Impatience, impulsiveness, and simply the wrong timing.

THE POWER OF THE PAUSE

Paul Harvey's radio broadcast is a rapid-fire mix of good news and bad, punctuated with dramatic and well-timed pauses. The halting delivery might communicate humor one moment and serious emotion the next. It's a good example of how silence can sometimes speak more powerfully than words.

James Dobson often uses a variation of this tactic in his own meetings. While he makes the most of every minute, he appreciates the value of giving colleagues as much of his time as the schedule permits. He never talks over a colleague or shuts down a discussion. If someone considers a comment worthy of speaking, the conversation deserves a hearing.

Del Tackett recalls that many of the weekly executive meetings could sometimes stretch as long as five hours because the boss always made sure everyone had his or her say. He was also a believer in striking when the iron was hot. If a situation regarding an employee came up and resolution required this person's perspective, Jim Dobson was famous for dealing with it then and there. "Well," he'd say, matter-of-factly, "let's get him in here right now and talk about it!" Quick and preemptive action often prevents a sticky situation from turning into a chronic problem.

A PROPER PERSPECTIVE

When people find out that I work directly for Dr. Dobson, it's not unusual for me to be peppered with questions. Most ask how he handles the dangers that accompany his high-profile position. Some of the popular questions include, "Does he have a security detail?" "Does he have a chauffeur?" "I hear his car is bulletproof . . . is that true?" "Does he go to restaurants?" (Incidentally, the answers to those questions are yes, no, no, and yes!)

While allowing him the privilege of privacy by limiting my remarks, I do see these very common questions as a grand opportunity to illustrate how good a grip the Dobsons have on God's sovereignty over their lives. Living in the public spotlight can be dangerous, especially when you have the courage to stick your neck out at a time when most are cowering in a corner. Yet Bruce Hoover, Dr. Dobson's chief of security, describes a man who, while cautious, is never overly concerned with matters pertaining to his personal welfare. When a recent death threat was received at Focus headquarters, Jim Dobson's schedule didn't skip a beat. While not one to take a foolish risk, he knows where he's going, so he's not going to spend a great deal of time looking over his shoulder to see where he's been or who might be following. "Jim Dobson won't scratch and claw out another day if today is his day to die. When the clock is out—it's out," says Del Tackett.

STEPPING OFFSTAGE

The pursuit of good timing is, of course, inextricably linked to following God's will, not man's plan. When we live in accordance with His plans as opposed to our own, we'll never risk overstaying our welcome or leaving before the job is complete.

I sat across from Dr. Dobson on a Monday morning in March 2003. We were discussing the topics of upcoming newsletters. Since he was headed to London for most of the summer to write, we were planning as far ahead as we could in order to minimize the distractions once he was on the other side of the Atlantic. I had come prepared with some suggestions but was surprised when he waved off my first idea for the May letter.

"No," he explained, "I'm reserving the May letter for a special announcement." Of course, I was intrigued. "Really!" I replied. "What might that be?"

"Please keep this confidential," he continued, "but I'm submitting my resignation as president of Focus on the Family effective May 15." My jaw nearly stubbed my toe. "I'm still going to be around," he assured me, "but the Lord has just presented us with a magnificent plan that I would never have dreamt possible only last year." As I listened, I couldn't help but consider that history was unfolding before my very eyes. Here was a man who had personally birthed an organization and nurtured it like his own child for twenty-six years. Yet, without hesitation, he seemed to be letting it go without struggle or strife. I could see that this was just another example of good timing. Following is a short portion of that May letter detailing his decision:

> For at least the past five years, we have been asking the Lord what He wanted of us in the days ahead. We were looking for guidance about "what comes next." Would it be retirement, or a reduced schedule, or an entirely different area of responsibility? We were open to anything the Lord might have for us, but He didn't do much talking. Every time we approached Him about the future, He has seemed to say succinctly, "Stay where you are until I tell you to move." Period! We took that to mean that

we were exactly where He wanted us to be, and that He would give us more specific directions when it was time for a change. So we stayed on the job, at Focus and at the National Day of Prayer, working up to ten or twelve hours a day, six days a week. Frankly, the load seemed backbreaking at times.

Now the Lord has spoken again, not audibly, but unmistakably. He has not told us to "move on"—but to "move over." That is what this transition is all about. Our compassionate Father has sent us a highly skilled colleague to help us handle the responsibilities. I'm reminded in this instance of the story told in the 18th chapter of Exodus (v. 17-23), when Moses was exhausting himself. His father-in-law, Jethro, came to visit him and observed the heavy burden that Moses was carrying. These are excerpts of what he said on that occasion:

> What you are doing is not good. You and these people who come to you will only wear yourselves out. The work is too heavy for you; you cannot handle it alone. Listen now to me and I will give you some advice, and may God be with you. . . . Select capable men from all the people—men who fear God, trustworthy men who hate dishonest gain—and appoint them as officials. . . . That will make your load lighter, because they will share it with you. If you do this and God so commands, you will be able to stand the strain, and all these people will go home satisfied.

I have no doubt that God ordained and orchestrated even the seemingly insignificant details surrounding this transfer of responsibility. Years earlier, Don Hodel had made a promise to the Lord that if he and Barbara were able, they would donate significant time and effort to ministry work. That day had arrived, and because the Dobsons sought to sync their watches with the Lord's, they've been able to step into God's plan and follow His perfect will.

James Dobson is not retired. He still comes in to the office every day. But now he's free to devote greater energy to his writing, broadcasting, and public policy responsibilities. He talks regularly to senators, congressmen, the White House, and ministry leaders around the country.

Dr. Dobson felt that God was not only asking him to "move over," but wanted him to model for other founders and presidents how to step down. Many people hang on too long and become a barrier to growth and effectiveness. Ego is the problem, because they don't want to give up their power. Solomon said in the book of Ecclesiastes, however, that there is a time for everything under the heavens, and certainly there is a time to relinquish authority in a Christian ministry. That time had come for Jim Dobson, and he wanted to submit to it.

POINTS TO REMEMBER

★ Bad timing can compromise good content. Consider the value of the three *B*'s: Be brief. Be bright. Be gone!

★ Appreciate the power behind the pause and simple silence. Both can speak more eloquently and articulately than all the words in the world.

★ Remember the sovereignty of the Supreme Master. If you forget that God protects His plans and His people, caution can easily turn into cowardice.

★ The wise begin to see the end in the beginning and continuously listen for direction from the Lord for when to move on.

PRACTICAL PRINCIPLE #19

BE THERE!

*Now is our chance to choose the right side. God is
holding back to give us that chance. It won't last
forever. We must take it or leave it.*

C. S. LEWIS

Since the early days of our courtship, my wife, Julie, and I have
enjoyed watching together the highly charged partisan debates
on various cable network news programs. We're admitted FOX
News fanatics and will literally holler at the set when a guest
stonewalls, filibusters, or tries to spin a response.

A direct answer to a question is a rare occurrence these days.
Truth has become increasingly relative, and cleverly worded responses are the norm. (Consider President Bill Clinton's infamous statement, "It depends on what the meaning of the word
'is' is.") Yet despite, or perhaps because of, this troublesome
trend, there is growing demand for those who will speak their
piece regardless of the price.

Dr. James Dobson is one such man. But not only does he
answer the questions asked of him, he also asks the critical questions that so many are afraid to ask themselves.

THE BOTTOM LINE

For the past thirteen years, Dr. Dobson's ninety-second radio
commentaries have been the third-most popular feature on the

dial, ranking behind only Paul Harvey's and Rush Limbaugh's short morning vignettes. Packed with poignant and powerful illustrations of such topics as marriage, family, and professional pursuits, his comments strike a chord with millions of listeners who wouldn't normally tune in to a "Christian" program.

Just prior to joining Dr. Dobson's personal staff, I spent three years syndicating this very feature and in doing so saw the impact it had on listeners as well as many of the radio executives who agreed to carry the program.

As an aside, I must tell you that the world of secular television and radio is a tough business with high-paced executives whose two main professional goals revolve around ratings and the procurement of advertising dollars. At first glance, one might assume there wouldn't be an overwhelming response for an avowed Christian conservative who unabashedly speaks about his love for the Lord and its influence in every aspect of his life. Yet many in the secular media business do respect both Dr. James Dobson and what he stands for. They listen when he talks. He is admired and accepted not only because of what he believes, but because he's not afraid of a tough question and he's not afraid to give a straight answer.

A few years ago, Al Peterson, editor of the leading trade publication *Radio & Records,* invited Dr. Dobson to address the annual Talk Radio Seminar in Washington, D.C. It was a high honor that Jim Dobson gratefully accepted. Having recently suffered and recovered from a major stroke, he decided to tackle as his topic what I would consider to be the ultimate questions and answers of life: "What gives my life meaning?" "Who really matters to me?" And finally, "Where do I find the answers to these questions?"

As we round the corner and spy the finish line, these insightful questions—and his answers—strike me as the ideal conclusion to our study of the personal and professional qualities of Dr. James Dobson.

After some introductory remarks and an explanation of the miraculous turn of events surrounding his recovery, Dr. Dobson shared the following story with a room full of harried media executives.

Some years ago, I struck up a friendship with the former basketball great Pete Maravich. He had recently become a Christian and was just on fire for the Lord. You couldn't talk with him for five minutes without him telling you about the difference Jesus Christ had made in his life. Pete had recently written a book entitled Heir to a Dream, *and he came out to California, where we were living at the time, to talk on our radio program about it.*

Back in those days, my friends and I used to play basketball three times a week, and on the morning of the interview, we had invited Pete Maravich to join us.

It was an audacious thing to do. "Pistol Pete," as he was dubbed by the media, had been one of the greatest basketball players of all time. He was the Michael Jordan or the Magic Johnson of his day. He set more than forty NCAA college records at Louisiana State University, many of which still stand. After graduation, Pete was drafted by the National Basketball Association and became the first player ever to receive a million-dollar contract. When he retired because of knee problems, he was elected to the NBA Hall of Fame the first year he was eligible. There is very little that can be done with a basketball that Pete Maravich didn't accomplish.

So for a bunch of "duffers" to invite a superstar like Pete to play with us took some gall, even though he was forty years old at the time. To our delight, he agreed to come and showed up at 7 AM. I quickly learned that he had been suffering from an unidentified pain in his right shoulder for many months. Aside from playing in the NBA Legends Game, which was televised nationally, Pete had not been on a basketball court in more than a year. Nevertheless, we had a good time that morning. Pete moved at about one-third his normal speed, and the rest of us huffed and puffed to keep up. We played for about forty-five minutes and then took a break to get a drink. Pete and I stayed on the court and talked while waiting for the other players to come back.

"You can't give up this game, Pete," I said. "It has meant too much to you through the years."

"You know, I've loved playing this morning," he replied. "I really do want to get back to this kind of recreational basketball. But it wouldn't have been possible in the last few months. The pain in my shoulder has been so intense that I couldn't have lifted a two-pound ball over my head."

"How are you feeling today?" I asked.

"I feel great," he said.

Those were Pete's last words. I turned to walk away, and for some reason looked back in time to see him go down. His face and body hit the boards hard. Still, I thought he was teasing. Pete had a great sense of humor, and I assumed that he was playing off his final comment about feeling good.

I hurried over to where Pete lay and still expected him to get up laughing. But then I saw that he was having a seizure. I held his tongue to keep his air passage open and called for the other guys to come help me. The seizure lasted about twenty seconds, and then Pete stopped breathing. We started CPR immediately but were never able to get another heartbeat or another breath. Pistol Pete Maravich, one of the world's greatest athletes, died there in my arms at forty years of age.

An autopsy revealed a few days later that Pete had a congenital malformation of the heart and never knew it. That was why his shoulder had been hurting. Whereas most of us have two coronary arterial systems that wrap around the heart, Pete only had one. How he was able to do such incredible exploits on the basketball court for so many years is a medical mystery. He was destined to drop dead at a fairly young age, and only God knows why it happened during the brief moment when his path crossed mine.

The shock of Pete's untimely death is impossible to describe. None of the men who witnessed the tragedy will ever forget it.

It is important to know something about Pete's background to understand who he was. Quite frankly, he had been a troublemaker when he was younger. He was a heavy drinker who broke all the rules. His attitude deteriorated in the NBA, and he finally quit in a huff. This man who had received every acclaim that can come to an athlete hit the skids emotionally. After retirement, he stayed in his house day after day to avoid autograph-seeking fans and because he had nowhere to go. There he sat, depressed and angry, for two years.

Something incredible happened at that crucial moment in Pete's life. He was in bed one night when he heard someone speak his name. He sat upright, wondering if he had been dreaming. Then he heard the voice again. Pete realized that God was calling him. He immediately knelt beside his bed and gave his heart to the Lord. It was a total consecration of his mind, body, and soul.

For the last five years of his life, all he wanted to talk about was what Jesus Christ had done for him. He told that story to reporters, to coaches, to fans, and to anyone who would listen. The day Pete died, he was wearing a T-shirt that bore the inscription, "Looking unto Jesus."

I was able to share that testimony with the media, which took it around the world within an hour. "You think Pete's great love was basketball," I told them, "but that was not his passion. All he really cared about was Jesus Christ and what He had done in Pete's life." And now I'm relaying that message to you. Perhaps that is why the Lord placed this good man in my arms as his life ebbed away.

Hitting Close to Home

Now I need to tell you something highly personal that happened next. I went home and sat down with our son, Ryan, who was seventeen years old at the time. I asked to talk to him about something of extreme importance to us both.

I said, "Ryan, I want you to understand what has happened here. Pete's death was not an unusual tragedy that has happened to only one man and his family. We all must face death sooner or later and in one way or another. This is the human condition. It comes too early for some people and too late for others. But no one will escape, ultimately. And, of course, it will also happen to you and me. So without being morbid about it, I want you to begin to prepare yourself for that time.

"Sooner or later, you'll get the kind of phone call that Mrs. Maravich received today. It could occur ten or fifteen years from now, or it could come tomorrow. But when that time comes, there is one thought I want to leave with you. I don't know if I'll have an opportunity to give you my 'last words' then, so let me express them to you right now. Freeze-frame this moment in your mind, and hold on to it for the rest of your life. My message to you is Be there! *Be there to meet your mother and me in heaven. We will be looking for you on that resurrection morning. Don't let anything deter you from keeping that appointment.*

"Because I am fifty-one years old and you are only seventeen, as many as fifty years could pass from the time of my death to yours. That's a long time to remember. But you can be sure that I will be searching for you just inside the Eastern Gate. This is the only thing of real significance in your life. I care what you accomplish in the years to come, and I hope you make good use of the great potential the Lord has given to you. But

above every other purpose and goal, the only thing that really matters is that you determine now to be there!"

That message is not only the most valuable legacy I could leave to Ryan and his sister, Danae, it is also the heart and soul of what I have tried to convey in this afternoon. Be there! This must be our ultimate objective in living. Within that two-word phrase are answers to all the other questions we have posed.

Jesus Christ is the source—the only source—of meaning in life. He provides the only satisfactory explanation for why we're here and where we're going. Because of this good news, the final heartbeat for the Christian is not the mysterious conclusion to a meaningless existence. It is, rather, the grand beginning to a life that will never end.

That same Lord is waiting to embrace and forgive anyone who comes to Him in humility and repentance. He is calling your name, just as He called the name of Pete Maravich. His promise of eternal life offers the only hope for humanity.

With these words, Dr. James Dobson bid the audience farewell and left to a standing ovation. It was a remarkable moment given the nonreligious nature of the event. The audience had arrived expecting a few simple words of professional encouragement and left with a bold and profound challenge to consider.

Dr. Dobson finds it impossible to separate his worship of the Lord from the work of his hands. Each of the principles discussed on the preceding pages flows from this foundation of fervent faith. It is the compass by which he steers. It is his North Star—immovable, unshakable, permanent. However honorable the other eighteen qualities may be, they are insignificant unless they're developed and utilized in tandem with the wisdom of God and the acceptance of his Son.

No matter your level of professional or personal pursuit, the most important thing you can do is to arrange life's priorities according to the standards of the King who came as a carpenter over two thousand years ago. He is the personification of perfection, the finest example of excellence in all the world.

May His eternal and timeless wisdom guide your steps, however steep or slippery your path may be.

THE FINAL WORD

JAMES C. DOBSON, PH.D.

Let us cross over the river and rest under the shade of the trees.
STONEWALL JACKSON

INTERNATIONALLY SYNDICATED TELEVISION HOST LARRY KING HAS HAD DR. JAMES DOBSON AS HIS GUEST ON BOTH RADIO AND TELEVISION FOR MORE THAN TWENTY YEARS. IN 2003, HE ASKED DR. DOBSON TO CONTRIBUTE A CHAPTER TO HIS NEW BOOK, *REMEMBER ME WHEN I'M GONE*. HE COMPLIED, BUT THEN THE OFFER WAS WITHDRAWN AFTER MR. KING RECEIVED A LARGE VOLUME OF HATE MAIL FROM HOMOSEXUAL ACTIVISTS WHO WERE UPSET OVER ONE OF DR. DOBSON'S APPEARANCES ON *LARRY KING LIVE*. THIS IS WHAT WOULD HAVE BEEN INCLUDED IN KING'S BOOK, BUT NOW IT SEEMS EVEN MORE FITTING AS A CONCLUSION TO *GADZOOKS!*

When I am asked how I want to be remembered at the end of life, my first reaction is to wonder why it matters. Who would really care? Future generations are unlikely to give a hoot. They will have preoccupations and challenges of their own and will spend precious little time admiring the relics of days gone by. It is rather foolish for us to think otherwise. Consider how few people alive today even know the names of their eight great-grandparents who died before they were born. Only a handful can cite anything substantive about their personalities, values, hopes, and dreams, even though these close relatives lived just a few decades ago. Clearly, the past is the past. May it rest in peace.

The wisest man who ever lived, King Solomon of ancient Israel, said it best: "For the wise man, like the fool, will not be long remembered; in days to come both will be forgotten" (Ecclesiastes 2:16). Solomon probably got this understanding from his father, King David, who wrote: "As for man, his days are like grass, he flourishes like a flower of the field; the wind blows over it and it is gone, and its place remembers it no more" (Psalm 103:15-16). From this perspective, I have concluded that it isn't important that I be remembered at all, except by a few friends and family members whom I love.

This concept of the brevity and impermanence of life has significantly influenced my thinking, going back to the early days of my professional experience. For fourteen years, I was a professor of pediatrics at the University of Southern California School of Medicine. Toward the end of that tenure, one of my colleagues died suddenly of an aneurysm. He had served on our medical faculty for more than a quarter of a century and earned the respect and admiration of both professionals and patients. This doctor had reached the pinnacle of success in his chosen field and enjoyed the status and financial rewards that accompany such accomplishment. He had tasted every good thing, by the standards of society.

At the next staff meeting following his death, a five-minute eulogy was read by a member of his department. Then the chairman invited the entire staff to stand, as is our custom in situations of this nature, for one minute of silence in memory of the fallen colleague. I have no idea what the other members of the staff were thinking during that sixty-second pause, but I can tell you what was going through my mind.

I breathed this silent prayer: *Lord, is this what it all comes down to? We sweat and worry and labor to achieve a place in life, to impress our fellow men with our competence. We take ourselves so seriously, overreacting to the insignificant events of each passing day. Then finally, even for the brightest among us, all these experiences fade into history and our lives are summarized with a five-minute eulogy and sixty seconds of silence. It hardly seems worth the effort.*

But I was also struck that evening by the collective inadequacy of that faculty to deal with the questions raised by our friend's death: Why was he born? Where had he gone? Would he live again? Will we see him on the other side? Were his deeds observed and recorded by a loving God? Is that God interested in me? Is there meaning to life beyond investigative research and professorships and big houses and expensive automobiles? The silent response of two hundred and fifty learned men and women seemed to symbolize our inability or unwillingness to grapple with those eternal questions.

I have continued to ponder the meaning of life as related to my own personal circumstances and especially the achievements of a lifetime that will be most highly prized when my days on this earth are growing short. In those final hours, will I be most proud of the plaques that hang on my wall or the awards I have been given or the degrees that I earned or the books I have written or the money I have accumulated through the years? Is this what I hope people will recall after I'm gone? I think not. There has to be greater substance to my reason for living than mere accomplishments and honors. Again, most of these successes will continue to have significance for a very short time.

I have already lived long enough to see some of my early dreams of glory come unstitched. One of them began shortly after I graduated from high school and went off to college. I arrived on campus several days before classes started and walked around looking at the place that would be my home for the next four years. I was like a tourist on holiday.

Of greatest interest to me that morning was the trophy case

standing in the main administration building. There behind the glass were the glitzy symbols of past athletic victories. Basketball, track, and baseball were well represented there. Then I saw it. Standing majestically at the center of the case was the perpetual tennis trophy. It was about two feet tall and had a shiny little bronze man on top. Engraved on the shaft were the names of all the collegiate tennis champions dating back to 1947. The identity of every one of those heroes was burned into my memory. I could name most of them today.

As I stood there before that historic trophy, I said to myself, *Someday! Some fine day I'm going to add my name to that list of legends.* I set my jaw and determined to show the world.

As ridiculous as it may seem today, becoming our college tennis champ was my highest goal in living at that time. Nothing could have mattered more to me. Tennis had been my passion in high school. I had played six days a week and eleven months a year. When I graduated and headed for college, it was my intention to ride this athletic talent into the record books.

Indeed, I did enjoy a certain amount of success in my tennis career. I lettered all four years, captained the team as a senior, and yes, I got my name inscribed on the big trophy. In fact, I did it twice during each of my last two seasons. I left the college with the satisfaction of knowing that future generations of freshmen would stand at the display case and read my name in admiration. Someday they might be great like me.

Alas, about fifteen years later a friend visited the campus of the college I had attended. He was dumping something in the trash behind the administration building, and what do you suppose he found? Yep, there amid the garbage and debris was the perpetual tennis trophy! The athletic department had actually thrown it away! What a blow! There I was, a legend in my own time, and who cared? Some universities retire the numbers on the jerseys of their greatest athletes. My school didn't retire my number. It retired my entire memory!

The father of the man who rescued my trophy had been one of my teammates in college, Dr. Wil Spaite. He took it home and cleaned it up. He put a new shiny man on the top and placed it on a new base that bore my name. Then he gave the refurbished trophy to me to commemorate my "prime," which everyone appeared to have forgotten. It stands in my office today. I'll show it to you if you come by for a visit. My name is inscribed there twice. You'll be impressed. It was a big deal at the time. Honest.

This brief encounter with fame taught me a valuable lesson about success and achievement. If we live long enough, life will trash my trophies—and yours, too. I don't care how important something seems at the time, if it is an end in itself, the passage of time will render it old and tarnished. Who cares today that James Polk or William Henry Harrison won their elections for president of the United States? Most students know nothing about them. Can you name three U.S. senators from the year 1933? Probably not, and why does it matter, anyway? What difference does it make that the Brooklyn Dodgers defeated the Yankees in the 1955 World Series? The hero of that series, Sandy Amoros, made a game-saving catch that a nation cheered, but he was soon penniless, forgotten, and living on the streets.

John Gilbert was the biggest romantic male movie star of the 1920s. He was by far the highest-paid actor in Hollywood, and his name was given top billing in every movie in which he starred. Almost everyone in the country knew his name. But within two years, no studio would hire him. Gilbert died in 1936 from a heart attack brought on by alcohol and drug abuse. He was just thirty-six years old. Have you ever heard of him? Probably not.

Let me share one more example. In the 1930s, one of the most famous men in the entire world was a man named Dr. Hugo Eckener. He was the German developer of the huge dirigibles (today we call them blimps) that had captured the imagination of people everywhere. Dr. Eckener was as well-known as Charles Lindbergh, Calvin Coolidge, and Charlie Chaplin. But no one remembers him today, except those who have studied the history of flight. His trophies are in the trash—and so are his dirigibles.

Well, here's the bottom line: Since all of our exhilarating accomplishments are going to fade and burn eventually, what *is* worth the investment of a lifetime? If those successes and achievements are of no lasting significance, then what will stand the test of time? I can speak only for myself, of course. After thinking through the issues I have raised today, everything seems to come down to this simple statement that I wrote twenty-seven years ago:

> I have concluded that the accumulation of wealth, even if I could achieve it, is an insufficient reason for living. When I reach the end of my days, a moment or two from now, I must look backward on something more meaningful than the pursuit of houses and land and machines and stocks and bonds. Nor is fame of any lasting benefit. I will consider my earthly existence to have been wasted unless I can recall a loving family, a consistent investment in the lives of people, and an earnest attempt to serve the God who made me. Nothing else makes much sense.

So how do I want to be remembered? Only as a man who lived by the creed stated above and then went on to heaven after doing his best as a flawed human being to please his Lord and Savior, Jesus Christ.

That is all.

That is enough.

APPENDIX

KEEP IT SIMPLE, KEEP IT SHORT

Dr. Dobson is a big fan of acronyms when corresponding with the staff via memo. Just for fun, here are some of his favorites:

OFFICE LINGO

LMSI . . . . Let Me See It

OYS . . . . Over Your Signature

OYS OMB . . . . Over Your Signature On My Behalf

OMS . . . . Over My Signature

MIG . . . . Make It Good

MAF . . . . Make A Friend

MUF . . . . Marriage Under Fire

IS . . . . Institutional Stench

Hot . . . . Please hurry

Hot Hot Hot . . . . Please hurry, hurry, hurry

Hottest . . . . Please hurry or you're fired!

TY . . . . Thank You

TBNT . . . . Thanks, But No Thanks

CACC . . . . Catch As Catch Can (Do it when circumstances permit)

YCT . . . . You Can Try

BOOK TITLES

STTM . . . . *Straight Talk to Men*

HS . . . . *Hide or Seek*

DD . . . . *Dare to Discipline*

WGDMS . . . . *When God Doesn't Make Sense*

WWW . . . . *What Wives Wish Their Husbands Knew about Women*

PIFC . . . . *Parenting Isn't for Cowards*

SWC . . . . *The Strong-Willed Child*

DDAYQ . . . . *Dr. Dobson Answers Your Questions*

LMBT . . . . *Love Must Be Tough*

CAR . . . . *Children at Risk*

BUB . . . . *Bringing Up Boys*

BUG . . . . *Bringing Up Girls (not yet published)*

LFAL . . . . *Love for a Lifetime*

TNSWC . . . . *The New Strong-Willed Child*

CHAPTER 3
[1] Paul Harvey, *Remember These Things* (Chicago: The Heritage Foundation, 1952), 18.

CHAPTER 5
[2] http://www.markdawg.com/sayings/sayingsn.html.

CHAPTER 6
[3] Proverbs 8:12-14

CHAPTER 11
[4] Al Lewis, "Memo to Employers: Cut Some Slackers," *The Denver Post* (January 30, 2004): C1.
[5] Russell Shaw, "Net Use at Work Spikes—and So Do Worries," Gannett News Service (October 21, 2002).

CHAPTER 12
[6] http://www.manteno.k12.il.us/finearts/advocacy/behavior.html

CHAPTER 14
[7] Robert Rhodes James et al., *Winston S. Churchill: His Complete Speeches, 1897–1963* (Broomall, Penn.: Chelsea House Publishers, 1979).

CHAPTER 16
[8] Lewena Bayer and Karen Mallett, "The Etiquette Ladies," *Lifewise,* http://www.canoe.ca/LifewiseWorkEtiquette/home.html.

CHAPTER 17
[9] Ravinder Mamtani, "Laughter Can Be Good for Your Health," *Poughkeepsie Journal* (August 17, 2003): B9.

CHAPTER 18
[10] Bob Cohn, "Not So Golden Oldies; Too Many Aging Jocks Won't Quit," *The Washington Times* (August 7, 2003): C1.
[11] Diana McCabe, "Timely Investing Tactics," *The Orange County Register* (May 12, 2002): D1.

Visit

ChristianBookGuides.com

for a discussion guide and other book
group resources for *Gadzooks!*